Psychology Revivals

More About Psychiatry

Originally published in 1951, *More About Psychiatry* invites readers deeper into the evolving world of psychiatry. Writing with clarity, compassion, and a deep respect for the human mind, Binger demystifies the psychiatric profession for the general reader, offering insights into the emotional and psychological struggles that shaped people's lives at the time.

Drawing on real-world cases and decades of clinical experience, Binger explores the roots of mental illness, the role of the psychiatrist, and the therapeutic relationship between doctor and patient. He addresses common misconceptions, the impact of early life experiences, and the growing importance of mental health in modern society. Today it can be read in its historical context.

This book is a re-issue originally published in 1951. The language used is a reflection of its era and no offence is meant by the Publishers to any reader by this re-publication.

More About Psychiatry

Carl Binger

Routledge
Taylor & Francis Group
LONDON AND NEW YORK

First published in Great Britain in 1951
by George Allen & Unwin Ltd

This edition first published in 2026 by Routledge
4 Park Square, Milton Park, Abingdon, Oxon, OX14 4RN

and by Routledge
605 Third Avenue, New York, NY 10158

Routledge is an imprint of the Taylor & Francis Group, an informa business

Publisher's Note
The publisher has gone to great lengths to ensure the quality of this reprint but points out that some imperfections in the original copies may be apparent.

Disclaimer
The publisher has made every effort to trace copyright holders and welcomes correspondence from those they have been unable to contact.

A Library of Congress record exists under LCCN: 52033888

ISBN: 978-1-041-19173-5 (hbk)
ISBN: 978-1-003-71042-4 (ebk)
ISBN: 978-1-041-19174-2 (pbk)

Book DOI 10.4324/9781003710424

More About Psychiatry

CARL BINGER

M. D.

Nature is unity ; the frontiers in
nature are erected by mankind.

CLAUDE BERNARD

London

GEORGE ALLEN & UNWIN LTD

Ruskin House, Museum Street

FIRST PUBLISHED IN GREAT BRITAIN
IN 1951

PRINTED IN GREAT BRITAIN
BY BRADFORD AND DICKENS,
LONDON, W.C.I.

TO

ARTHUR H. RUGGLES, M.D.

for His Friendship and Wisdom

Foreword

OUR thoughts are like winged insects. They have their shimmering day. When we impale them on a pen point, they soon lose their apparent brilliance. Yet we lay them out for others to see, and we look at them ourselves, perhaps with the hope of recapturing their original sheen. But they have a way of graying out. Most of us say the same thing over and over again, but each resaying helps us to understand our own ideas, born often only in the saying or in the writing.

The chapters in this book were first presented, for the most part, as addresses to audiences composed of doctors or medical students; some were addressed to laymen; and a few, to mixed groups. Certain of them were written as articles in magazines and one as part of a textbook. Due acknowledgment of permission to publish them is made elsewhere in this volume.

In talking about one's own specialty, it is easy to slip into cant, more difficult to be clear and nontechnical. I have tried not to be oversimple or yet "to gild the philosophic pill." If this book reaches some medical students and physicians, I shall be satisfied, but it may interest social workers as well and those members of the lay public who are aware of medicine as a growing and changing body of knowledge. I have attempted to indicate certain directions of its growth; there are, of course, many others.

A collection of essays or of lectures runs the risk of being ponderous and of creaking at the joints like the mechanical man who plays chess at the wax works. If I have succeeded, and I hope that I have, in breathing life into this one, it is because it represents a kind of record of my daily experiences. Since these experiences have to do with the puzzling problems that beset every physician, the effort to tackle them and to find solutions for them perhaps will give the book continuity enough. It was not carefully planned. My wife says, of my literary efforts, that I behave as if I were a ghost writer to a volcano. But after the eruption, when the flow of lava has cooled off, I try to pick my way through the debris. Then I strive to follow the advice that Alexander Pope gave to the poets when he told them that they should "compose with fury but correct with phlegm."

I find now that the chapters, as arranged, fall into several general groups: The first four are concerned with various aspects of psychosomatic medicine, more specifically with the relationship of the emotions to bodily disturbances. Then there is a chapter called "What Can We Learn from a Medical History?" that links medicine and psychiatry. This is followed by three chapters of more definitely psychiatric content. These, in turn, lead up to another transitional chapter called "What Is Mental Health?" serving as an introduction to the last five, which branch out from a concern with the individual to a concern with the community and with the world situation.

Many people to whom I am grateful helped in the preparation of this book: audiences who have tolerated me, patients who have taught me, students who have stimulated me. There are also several whom I wish especially to thank: Mrs. Ruth Potter Duell for advice in selecting and editing the material; Mrs. Charlotte Lieman, my secretary, for indefatigable typing and retyping of manuscript; Dr. Henry Alden Bunker, my old friend and literary conscience; Dr. Lyman Bryson, Mr. Lloyd K.

Garrison, Dr. Horace Gray, Dr. Margaret Mead, Dr. Henry A. Murray, and Dr. Thomas A. C. Rennie, each of whom has read and given me valuable criticism on one or more of the chapters.

C. B.

New York, New York

Acknowledgments

GRATEFUL acknowledgment for permission to reprint part or all of these essays is made to

The *Pharos* of Alpha Omega Alpha for chapter i.

The *American Scholar* for chapter ii.

Bulletin of the New York Academy of Medicine for chapters iii and iv.

The *American Journal of Medicine* for chapter v.

McCall Corporation for chapters vi, ix, and x.

Associated Magazine Contributors, Inc., for chapter vii.

Dr. Henry A. Christian and Oxford University Press for chapter viii.

Harper's Magazine and the *Cincinnati Journal of Medicine* for chapter xi.

Mental Hygiene for chapter xii.

The *American Journal of Orthopsychiatry* for chapter xiii.

International Congress for Mental Health and the *American Scholar* for chapter xiv.

Contents

CHAPTER I

The Doctor's Dilemma

I HAVE taken my title from *The Doctor's Dilemma*, the play of that name by George Bernard Shaw. Perhaps it should have been in the plural—dilemmas—rather than dilemma; for in Shaw's view there are plenty of them. It appears to him that we are lost in a forest of horns, struggling to extricate ourselves without too much damage to our self-esteem. G. B. S. was of course chiefly concerned with the social and economic problems of doctoring, of which we are hearing so much discussion today, but he did not hesitate to shoot his pointed darts at what he conceived to be our unscientific methods and our general incompetence. He inveighed against the perils of inoculation and the cruelties of vivisection and deported himself generally like the highhanded and highhearted gentleman he is. Still, it will do us no harm to take a quick look at ourselves in the Shavian mirror, even though it magnifies the blemishes of our complexion.

Here are some random pickings from his tart crop:

"Medical science is as yet imperfectly differentiated from common curemongering witchcraft."

"Their [the doctors'] reputations stand, like an African king's palace, on a foundation of dead bodies."

". . . the rank and file of doctors are no more scientific than their tailors."

And: "Doctoring is an art, not a science . . . not even the art of keeping people in health . . . it is the art of curing illness."

These diatribes were hurled at the profession forty years ago, and in his long life Shaw has relented very little. Other famous men of the past, Molière and Napoleon in particular, took pleasure in ridiculing us.

Today this attitude has changed. Thanks largely to the excellent publicity which scientific medical discovery has been given in the daily press and in magazine articles and to the educational activities of such organizations as the American Medical Association and the New York Academy of Medicine, the man in the street now expects his physician to be well trained in medical science and to keep abreast of the times. The enlightened layman is no longer content with a bottle of Brown's Mixture or rhubarb and soda, however saintly the hands of the administering physician. He is prepared to undergo fairly prolonged, and even expensive, examinations, in order that his doctor can make an accurate diagnosis. He is, moreover, interested in the diagnosis, likes to bandy medical terms—sometimes, to be sure, quite correctly pronounced. But his interest by no means ends with the establishing of a diagnosis and the affixing of a label on what he calls his "condition." And here the doctor's dilemma begins.

The doctor's interest, especially if he is carefully grounded in medical science, often flags just at this point—at the point where he is called upon to do something about the diagnosis he has so carefully and skilfully arrived at. This does not bespeak inhumanity in him or cold indifference to the discomfort or suffering of his patient. But the orderly process of gathering data, collating them, drawing inferences from them which affords him such intellectual satisfaction, no longer stands him in good stead when it comes to treatment. He must often resort to empirical, trial-and-error methods, to therapeutic procedures based on no sounder rationale than that they seem to work.

Here, then, is a sharp dilemma: All the sick man really wants is to get well by any method that works, but the modern doctor is suspicious of therapy not logically based on scientific observation and experiment. And even if such a method should work, he can espouse it with no enthusiasm and recommend it with no conviction. Skepticism is sufficient to keep an unscientific method from working. There can be little doubt that chiropractors and faith healers achieve cures by methods which would be worthless in our hands, because we do not understand them and, therefore, cannot believe in them. They treat the anxiety so prevalent in us by invoking a form of magic. It is something to give us pause that an irregular method, even a foolish method, can sometimes succeed where we fail. Our accustomed attitude toward these successes is first one of denial, then one of explaining them away. We try to convince Jones that he never could have had migraine, because we know that migraine results from a dilatation of the arteries branching off from the external carotid and, moreover, that it occurs most frequently in meticulous, overconscientious, rather compulsive individuals. Do not try to tell me that manipulating his spine and kneeling on the small of his back is going to alter the blood supply to Jones's meninges or change him into a carefree, relaxed, debonair person. But the fact is that, since going to his chiropractor, Jones no longer suffers from prostrating headaches for which we gave him injections of gynergen, after having failed with elimination diets, and injunctions to take things easy. Now what *can* this mean?

Are you recommending, you will say to me, that we scuttle the Ship of Science, that we finally yield to the constant push and pull to which we are daily subjected by our patients in their efforts to force us back into the role of magician, exorcist, and miracle worker? I hasten to say: "No—far from it—not at all." But I want to add this statement with all emphasis: the fact that quackery and charlatanry sometimes succeed when science fails is at the root of our dilemma and is in itself a fit subject for scientific inquiry. I believe that we have begun to understand, at least in part, the answer, which does not involve any magic or magician.

The blatant curemonger, as Shaw called him (I use the term without invidiousness), proceeds in some such fashion as this: He says to his patient: "This medicine which I am going to give you does not taste very nice, but it contains all the salts and vitamins which your starving tissues crave. It is made from carefully selected natural herbs and is not adulterated with poisonous animal proteins. It will, moreover, rebuild your wasted nervous tissue. You will find that it makes your eyes bright and your step springy and increases your energy. Do not expect to feel the effects at once; it may take several weeks."

The more this kind of healer is persuaded of the truth of his assertions, the more effective will be the suggestion which he conveys to his patient. We are all extremely susceptible to suggestion, as any advertising man can tell you.

Now a scientifically trained physician cannot compete with this sort of claptrap. Indeed, the more skeptical he is, the less will he be able to reinforce his therapy with such suggestion. And yet suggestion may be essential for cure. What is the way out of this impasse? The only one that I can see is to deal clinically with the problem of anxiety, which complicates all illness. Common sense and acumen are, of course, essential, but they are not enough. We need, in addition, specific scientific training in the dynamics of personality. We shall not then confuse ourselves and our patients by prescribing small doses of digitalis for "psychological reasons." But we will give digitalis in those quantities which the heart muscle requires, and we will no less specifically treat the psychological difficulty with planned and conscious psychological methods.

But what relevance have these remarks for a medical student or for a young physician working in a hospital? A hospital is a wonderful place where one can observe much about human relationships. It can be what Herman Melville said of the whaling ship, that it was his Harvard and his Yale. It is so easy to fall into the error against which Francis Peabody cautioned us, the error of depersonalizing our patients. Recall his wise remark: "The secret of the care of the patient is in caring for the patient." Do not think of Henry Jones as "that case of mitral stenosis in the second bed on the left." That is a most unscientific way (and also, incidentally, an inhuman way) of thinking about him. No man is a case of mitral stenosis or of pneumonia or even of schizophrenia. These labels are abstractions, hypotheses, fictions, if you will, which help us, as a certain philosopher once said, in the regulation of our errors so that we can "accept ever closer approximations to the unattainable reality." The reality is, in this instance, the suffering individual. It is he whom we must study to know.

Goethe said: "Man lernt nichts kennen als was man liebt" ("One understands only what one loves"). And Hippocrates: "Where the love of man is, there also is the love of the Arts."

Students of medicine, who are filled to overflowing with scientific facts, perhaps will lend only a scornful, if tolerant, ear to such sentiments. They belong to the generation of the tough-minded. They know all about the 17-ketosteroids, about the specific dynamic action of protein, about the vagaries of the T wave, and the P-R interval, about the Rh factor, splanchnicectomy, thiouracil, the electroencephalograph, about sulpha levels in the blood, and the various strains and races of pneumococci and streptococci. What truck have they with Goethe and Hippocrates and their talk of love—an emotion that cannot be weighed and measured?

I believe that this emotion is the power behind much of our therapy—specific as well as nonspecific. The crux of the doctor's dilemma is to bring this curative power under control. By a deeper understanding of his relationship with his patient the doctor will find the way out of his present dilemma, now best expressed by opposing the roles of *exact scientists* and of *healers*. But what do I mean by love? Naturally, I am not talking about romance, about amorousness, or eroticism, though even in nonpsychiatric medicine these elements may be latently present. On the doctor's part, they must never be more than latent. He should, at least, strive to recognize them for what they are and not allow himself to become too involved in his patient's emotional involvement with him or yet be cold to his needs.

To achieve this requires some self-knowledge, some capacity for introspection and for self-observation. These are qualities not greatly prized in our contemporary society, where the ideal citizen is expected to be a smiling "extravert" who never thinks about himself and seldom about anything else. But the doctor needs to think about these matters, if he wants to retain his scientific integrity and wants not to become a charlatan, however sincerely believing in his nonexistent knowledge and in his magical powers.

For these reasons, and others, great physicians from Hippocrates to Osler have been concerned with ethics and morality. It is a crass and callow view of medical science to think that concepts of good and evil can be dispensed with and that they are not intimately related to the condition of our health.

Surely Paracelsus must have had some such thoughts when he said: "The greatest and highest of all qualifications which a physician should possess is *Sapientia*—i.e., Wisdom—and without this qualification all his learning will amount to little or nothing as far as any benefit to humanity is concerned. . . ." "We cannot find wisdom in books," he said, "nor in any external things; we can only find it within ourselves."

Let me now take our dilemma into the clinic by referring it whence it came: to the individual patient and his concerns. If we want to retain the validity and to renew the vitality of our speculations, we have need constantly to refer them to their clinical sources. So we will take a case in which medicine as a biological science and medicine as a healing art may seem to be in conflict.

I should like to tell you about a patient—a twenty-two-year-old paratrooper. He fought in both the Pacific and the European theaters. He had been in the service for about two years. His military record was distinguished for his leadership and his cool intrepidity, but he was at continuous odds with his officers, whom he refused to salute. Indeed, on one occasion he was court-martialed for striking an officer. He entered and left the armed forces as a private, having refused promotion as well as a recommendation for officer's training. He also declined to accept the Purple Heart. I was consulted about this young man by a relative of his who told me the following story:

In the fall of 1945 he entered a civilian hospital to have a dislocated meniscus removed from his left knee. The injury to the knee had occurred while playing football a few years before his enlistment. On several occasions thereafter he "threw his knee out," as he expressed it, the last time in Germany, when, on night patrol and climbing a hill as quietly as possible, his knee "went out" before he got to the top of the hill, and he rolled to the bottom.

Following surgical removal of the meniscus under pentothal anesthesia, he was returned to the ward, where he slept quietly for seven hours. At about 4:30 P.M. of the same day the intern was summoned, only to find six medical students and several nurses struggling to hold him in bed. All attempts to quiet him with words or sedatives—including intravenous morphine sulphate—failed. It was finally necessary to hold him with leather restraints in order to prevent him from hurting himself and others. This violent delirious state continued intermittently all that night and throughout most of the next day—undoubtedly aggravated by cortical depression resulting from occasional injections of morphine. There were, however, lucid periods in which he was quiet, co-operative, and accurately oriented. On the following day he was fine and remained cheerful and happy throughout his convalescence.

Instead of looking upon this mishap as merely a troublesome nuisance, the intern made careful notes of what the patient said during his delirium. These notes and the subsequent history give some clue as to what was going on.

Let me give you a condensed account of the intern's record: All the statements which the patient made were clear and logical. There were basically three themes which he talked about: the war and football and his wife. Of the first the most striking element was the hate he had for his captain. He threatened to "kill him," "smash his face in," and "cut his throat." His chief grievance was that the captain would not go into battle with his men but stayed ten miles behind the lines. Here are some verbatim quotations from the young paratrooper's stream of talk, while under the influence of pentothal:

"I don't like mines," he said, "you don't know where they are. We'll flip a coin to see who goes first. Heads you go, tails I go. We got no coin? Toss your ration box; if it comes down right side up, you go; if it comes down right side down, I go. All right, you guys, you follow me—*and keep in single file*. That way only one of us gets hit—not two. Of course you're scared. I'm scared—*but we got to go.*"

While struggling violently against restraint, he shouted:

"Open that door. Let me out of here. Those poor devils are getting it—we're the second wave—open that door. We've been hit once already."

"I'm only a buck private, but I know. So don't you offer me a commission. I won't take it. It's no use—*I won't take it.*"

"You don't fight for the four freedoms. You fight for your life. Kill or be killed. Give me a knife, I'll get him. [Here he reached out and grabbed a percussion hammer from the intern's pocket but relinquished it without struggle.]

"*You* never cut a man's throat. You don't know what it feels like. Give me a Tommy gun. Don't give me a B.A.R. Think I want to stay three hundred yards away? Give me a Tommy."

All this was said with the most intense feeling, and the patient acted as if he were actually in battle. It is to be noted that he never once cursed.

Now as to his remarks about football, in which you will recall he originally sustained the injury to his knee. Here again he was giving instructions to the new boys. He played as earnestly as he fought, and he mentioned that he must not let on how badly his knee hurt.

"Dad said no, I had enough exercise anyway, said I wouldn't make my grades. I made better grades than ever. I threw my knee out playing football. I didn't say anything about it. Then I fell down the steps in the barn and threw it out again. I didn't lie. Don't know why Dad is like that. A few years ago I could have had my own farm, but Dad talked me out of it. Now I don't want to do anything. *Whenever I get home, seems like I always have accidents—break something.*" [This remark, as you will learn later, is of great significance. It offers the clue, not only to an extraordinary proneness to accidental injury, but to the life-situation and development of personality which lie behind this dangerous tendency.]

Then he went on: "I'll work for you, Dad—only don't tell me *how* to do it. I'll do it."

Of his wife he said little. He called her by name and once told her that he would ride a horse and did not care if his knee was hurt. In an apparently lucid moment when she tried to reassure him that his knee would be all right, he remarked: "Then I can go to work on the other one and smash that up."

So much for the data supplied by the intern. The patient remained in the hospital for nine days, when he returned to the home of the relative who had consulted me about him. There he was good-humored, loved a joke, and talked freely about farming, his training as a paratrooper, and other matters. He showed no apparent emotional disturbance.

I learned certain additional facts about him of which I shall present just a few significant ones. He was an only child; his mother died when he was ten years old. After her death, and in the impressionable years of prepuberty, he lived in close contact with his father—with few other companions. His father is a man of great charm—a forceful, dominating, often domineering person. The boy both admires him and resents him. Four years after his mother's death, his father remarried. The stepmother is devoted to the boy and often is forced into the role of arbiter between the two.

The tendency to suffer accidents began in his early

childhood; just when, I do not know—but apparently before his mother's death. Up to the present he has sustained twenty-two fractures: his jaw, several ribs, his clavicle, both hands—in bare fist fights—both legs, one foot—when he quite unnecessarily jumped into a cattle pen—and either a spinous process or transverse process of a vertebra. Of this injury to his back he said:

"The last thing Dad said to me that morning was—'Don't fall out of the tree.' I knew that branch was rotten, but I stepped on it anyway and it broke under my weight."

Many of his accidents have occurred after some altercation with his father, from whom he has been unable to separate himself. In spite of his intense hostility, he is seldom defiant. He will simply shut up like a clam, say nothing, and sullenly go back to work. Then a horse will kick him or a steer will trample on his foot. By ordinary standards he is a boy of excellent character and unusual personal charm. He neither drinks nor smokes. To date he has shown no significant depression. We have reason to believe that he joined the paratroopers with the hope of being killed. That he was aware of this may be inferred from a remark he made after his discharge from the hospital, to wit: that he hoped he would not come back; it would be a polite kind of suicide, and he might do some good in the meantime.

It is doubtful whether the underlying pattern of this lad's life would have come to light without the unintentioned release of repressed material set off by pentothal and morphine. A less comprehending intern would have looked upon the episode simply as a disturbance to ward routine.

Clearly this is one of a group of individuals who have been described as "accident-prone." That such a group exists is supported by statistical as well as psychological evidence. On the basis of studies carried out by the National Research Council it is estimated that 88–90 per cent of all industrial accidents seem to be related to something in the personality of the individual; and it is known statistically that the probability of having accidents is greater in the person who has had previous ones. By some concatenation of circumstances, such persons are led without awareness into situations resulting in their injury. It is amazing how often fate and outer reality seem to conform to their needs. One can only guess that some impairment of judgment, some delay in reaction time, some disturbance of kinesthetic or position sense or balance, results from the emotional conflicts in which they find themselves. The conflict which they have so much difficulty in resolving lies between their own independent spontaneity and the restrictive pressure of external authority with which they have never learned to cope.

I have mentioned their emotional needs. How can self-injury be a need? This would seem a contradiction in terms, but alas it is not. Without wishing now to enter too deeply into this aspect of the problem, it can be said that the accident itself—however inconvenient, painful, or dangerous—often does satisfy certain unconscious requirements. It is a penitent, self-punishing gesture, temporarily absolving the sufferer from the guilt of his hostile, even murderous, impulses. It is an emotionally parried thrust directed against the loved and hated person but deflected so that the dagger of Brutus strikes not Caesar but himself.

I began this chapter with some speculations about the apparent conflict between medicine as a biological science and medicine as a healing art. This conflict I called the doctor's dilemma. As a way out of it, I urged that the physician must acquire a deeper understanding not only of his patient but also of himself and of their mutual relationships. It is clear that no manipulative skill, however expert, no stereoscopic x-rays or Balkan frames or vitallium screws, will mitigate the accident habit or prevent its recurrence. This can only be done, if at all, by the application of the methods of science to understanding the patient's personality.

Let me now apply these generalizations to the patient whose life-history I have just related. May I say that I chose this particular one for several reasons. First the charge of malingering, so often leveled by the uninformed at the mentally or emotionally ill, can hardly be said to apply here. There is nothing in this history suggestive of conscious intent—nor had the patient any real insight into the inexorability of the unconscious mechanism at work in him. Second, the outmoded and, to my mind, specious dispute as between what is organic and what is functional does not hold here. A broken jaw or spinous process or a dislocated meniscus is an "organic" lesion. You may, of of course, quote the old adage: "Sticks and stones may break my bones, but names will never hurt me." True enough; but the ruin rained on Coventry and Nuremberg, on Pearl Harbor and Nagasaki, though actually the result of violent physical explosion, was born of political emotion at white heat. So in the body—it is the physical disturbances—the signs and symptoms—that we recognize as disease, but we are likely to overlook the emotional tensions which set these processes in motion or act as triggers to release prepared mechanisms.

In other bodily disorders, now called "psychosomatic," the connections between emotions and their physical manifestations are often less obvious than they were in the patient I have described. Such disturbances, for example, as ulcer, hypertension, and bronchial asthma are associated with derangements of secretion, motility and tone of smooth muscle. In all of them, impulses traveling along autonomic and sympathetic pathways influence the functioning of the effector organs. And in all of them it is believed that emotional tension, especially that generated by deeply repressed unconscious conflicts, escapes along these visceral pathways—just as grief escapes in tears.

If we were going to inquire into a relatively simple bodily process such, for example, as the shedding of tears, it is evident that no study of the electrolyte concentration of the tears themselves or of the morphological structure of the lachrymal glands or of the action current in the facial nerve, even if measured with a cathode ray oscillograph, could give us any information whatever about the mood of the person who was crying. To get such information, we should need quite different methods.

We might discover in one individual that weeping was a highly conditioned response to a certain set of circumstances: that, because of specific events in his past life, a stimulus which would be of no moment to one person opened the floodgates for another. Or, again, that in one, tears were the expression of sadness, in another of anger, in a third of joy, in a fourth of pain, or, in fact, of a mixture of emotions. If it were to our interest to stop the flow of tears or to prevent them, we could, of course, administer large doses of atropine, cut the appropriate branches of the facial nerves, or extirpate the lachrymal glands; or we could, by a long process of deconditioning and reeducation render the person less reactive to a particular stimulus.

After this rather long digression, let me return to the paratrooper. A third and most important reason for selecting him as an illustration is this one: Because from an administrative point of view it is actually a surgical, not a psychiatric, case. If the surgeon has no understanding of his patient's problems, there is not much likelihood of the patient's seeking help, unless he is overtaken by tragedy, such as severe depression, continued failure at his work, or disruption of his marriage. And even in these events, a patient such as this one will—in all probability—grimly go to it again and repeat his errors. Surgeons are busy men—they are objective in their approach, and, moreover, they have no time and no training to rummage around in the psyche. I am not recommending that they do—any more than that psychiatrists should rummage around in the peritoneal cavity. Perhaps the surgeon should, however, recognize when he is dealing with an emotionally disturbed person, just as the psychiatrist should know the difference between the pains due to terminal ileitis and those of hysterical conversion. The excuse of lack of time has never impressed me. There is no time not to know these things.

But assuming, as in this case, that the surgeon does spot the difficulty, how can he persuade so proud and defiant a lad to consult a psychiatrist? Only by utilizing to the utmost the confidence which his patient has in him. Here is where the doctor-patient relationship is of paramount importance. This boy, because of his ambivalent relationship to his father, has a highly conditioned set of emotional responses—a kind of one-way system—prepared and canalized by his past experience. He will inevitably make his physician into just such an authoritarian figure against whom he will rebel—perhaps not openly—but by sabotaging the treatment or by further self-injury. We physicians are traditionally placed in the role of fathers by our patients. We are loved and admired and worshiped by them and also criticized and feared and hated. Freud has called this attitude the transference, because it is one which actually belongs elsewhere—usually in childhood—but is transferred on to us. The handling of this relationship has become one of the chief tools—and one of the most difficult to manipulate—in modern psychotherapy. It is essential that we understand it if we are not to be enmeshed in the coils of our patients' emotional conflicts.

You will acknowledge that the therapeutic challenge which our hero presents to us is no slight one, and yet it is the quintessential one of psychosomatic medicine. We need to do more than to ask a patient whether there is anything on his mind or whether he and his wife are sexually compatible. We need to gain knowledge of the main structure of his personality: What are his underlying drives; how can they be released into productive and creative activities rather than into socially or physically destructive ones?

In every society there are rational and irrational elements, and these are reflected in its medicine—just as they were in ancient Greece by the medicine of the Hippocratic Schools and the medicine of the Aesculapian Temples.

It is the task of modern psychiatry to bring the rational to bear on the irrational. Only by fulfilment of this task will the physicians find the way out of the dilemma, for it is not one that exists in nature. It is man-made, deriving from our way of looking at nature. When we do so more inclusively, the apparent conflict between the science of medicine and the art of healing will vanish.

CHAPTER II

Psychosomatic Medicine

THE notion that the mind and body are closely related in their behavior is as old as medicine and philosophy. Aristotle and Hippocrates knew it; Paracelsus proclaimed it; and Jean Paul Marat elaborated upon it—he whose career as a brilliant and versatile physician ended before he took his tragic part in the French Revolution. But for the modern origins of what is now called "psychosomatic medicine" we must look to the Germany of the early eighteen hundreds—particularly to the work of Nasse (1778–1851) and Jacobi (1775–1858).

In America, Oliver Wendell Holmes, Sr., was alive to the effects of social and personal problems on health, but he judged his professional colleagues not yet ready to accept such ideas, so he dispensed them in the form of his three "medicated novels"—*Elsie Venner, A Mortal Antipathy*, and *The Guardian Angel*. Toward the close of the last century a Boston physician, Dr. Robert T. Edes, wrote *The New England Invalid*, a classical description of a familiar type of woman patient in whom emotional disturbances and physical symptoms coexist. A few years later Dr. James Jackson Putnam, the first professor of neurology at Harvard and one of the earliest Americans to come under the influence of Freud, wrote an article called "Not the Disease Only, but Also the Man."

These random historical items are straws pointing the wind. Many others could be found. In our own time and place it is Dr. George Draper who deserves credit for his emphasis on the "psychological panel" of human constitution. As early as 1928 he published a paper in the *Journal of the American Medical Association* with the title: "Disease, a Psysomatic Reaction." Later the more euphonious *cho* was inserted and the word "psychosomatic" came into being. It seems to have come to stay. It is not altogether a happy choice. Its synthetic form emphasizes the very division which it purports and pretends to unite. What the name should denote is that the mind and body are one, that there is no *psyche* without *soma* and no *soma* without *psyche*, that these labels apply to two aspects of a single life-process. And yet, by its implication, the term "psychosomatic" puts asunder what God hath joined together.

It is true for convenience we are obliged to separate the mind from the body because we still need quite different tools for studying them. We cannot scrutinize the emotions with a microscope or measure the blood flow through the kidneys by holding a sympathetic interview with them. But the purpose of this separation is to achieve a more complete view of man and his illnesses. We proceed as we did in the old-fashioned method of treating a split lip, which was to split it further—so that it would heal from the bottom up.

We are still far from such a goal. We have, in fact, no operational concept to test—no unifying hypothesis which bridges the gap between what is mind and what is body; no explanation of how they influence each other. It is not enough to say that the mind is the output of the functioning brain, as hydrochloric acid is the output of certain glands in the mucous lining of the stomach. There are those who believe that all mentation (perception, emotion, volition, etc.) *is* muscular activity. Such a view has the advantage of simplicity. To those holding it there is no cleft separating the psychic from the somatic. But it is an assertion still in need of proof.

The concept of a mind-stuff is another attempt to find a unifying principle. If there were a material substance with the properties of mind, governed by thermodynamic laws, then we could proceed with our observations on surer grounds. Psychology would be a physical science, the millennium around the corner, and the lion and the lamb at last comfortable bedfellows. But that is still in the nature of a pipe dream.

We are forced, therefore, to pursue each discipline, that is, the physiological and the psychological, with its own appropriate technic—striving always to establish correlations. We must not labor the argument of "causality." That is both foolish and premature and leads merely to a chicken-and-egg analogy.

In this field of psychosomatic medicine we are not dealing with such invariable relationships as might be expressed in the statement: *A* acting on *B* produces *C*. Illness is not always the immutable effect of some cause but rather the outcome of a process of development in which innumerable factors play a role. The same is true of such social phenomena as wars.

In studying illness, therefore, we do not restrict our investigations to a search for causes, but we analyze the processes by which individuals fall ill. When we do that, we will find that many of the illnesses, misadventures, even diseases, which men suffer are critically dependent upon a disturbance of their emotions.

There is nothing new in this thought. It was inherent in the ancient theory of the bodily humors. Roman matrons guessed at it when they measured their daughters' necks to detect in them an erotic adventure. (Many years passed before the reciprocal influence of ovaries and thyroid through the anterior portion of the pituitary gland was found to exist.)

When the Scottish surgeon, John Hunter (1728–93),

made his famous remark, "I am at the mercy of any rascal who causes me to lose my temper," and almost immediately thereafter, in a fit of rage, succumbed to a heart attack, he, too, knew what every wise physician has always realized: that profound emotions express themselves in bodily changes and may, indeed, be the trigger which sets off a great variety of symptoms—some slight, some serious.

If, then, this has always been known to doctors of medicine, why all the fuss about psychosomatic medicine? Why this twenty-five-dollar word? Why pour old wine into new bottles? Why organize a Society for Research in Psychosomatic Problems with about five hundred members? Why publish a periodical with a subscription list of some twenty-five hundred? Why print a series of monographs dealing with such subjects as bronchial asthma, peptic ulcer, colitis, and arterial hypertension?

Have we any new knowledge to justify all this activity? The truth is that we have—even if it is not yet all assimilated and organized. The twentieth century brought us, among others, three great scientists in the field of biology. Within the past few years all three have died: Walter B. Cannon, Ivan Pavlov, and Sigmund Freud. Cannon would have none of Freud, though he acknowledged Pavlov as his intellectual father. Pavlov forbade his laboratory workers to use psychological language. Dissatisfied with the term "psychic secretion" for describing the flow of saliva in dogs stimulated by the smell of food or by other signals, he invented the term "conditioned reflex." He insisted on sticking to his physiologist's last. Both he and Cannon shied away from the concept of an unconscious mind.

Not so Freud. Although trained as a physiologist and although himself a brilliant pupil of the French neurologist, Charcot, Freud turned his back on experimental biology. His laboratory was his study, his sole equipment a couch, his cats and dogs and guinea pigs—a suffering man. To think that his contribution is less mechanistic than the others is to misread him. He was interested primarily in mental mechanisms and in discovering the laws which govern them. He, therefore, examined such things as suppression and repression, projection, displacement, and conversion. His trenchant literary style, often a mixture of poetical and scientific phraseology, has caused him to be misjudged as less of an empirical scientist than he actually was, and it has, unfortunately, seduced some of his followers into a sterile scholasticism. But, like Prometheus, Freud was a Titan who gave us fire, and he was made to suffer for it.

The essence of his thought lies in the concept of an unconscious mind—the very thing that neither Cannon nor Pavlov would accept, because there was no experimental "proof" for its existence. To Freud, man was like an iceberg: only a relatively small portion of his mental life is visible above the surface of the water. Man's habits, his choices, his errors, his wit, his genius, his loves and hates, his sickness and his health, the institutions which he creates and the civilization in which he lives—all are, in large measure, shaped and determined by impulses arising from the "submerged" part of himself. Because of various prohibitions and restrictions on his behavior these impulses cannot always hit their mark. His rages do not all lead to murder. A state of tension arises in him, and he strives always to relieve this tension by finding some acceptable outlet for his unruly and uncivilized impulses. If he is lucky, he will learn, by a kind of trial-and-error method, to "sublimate" these impulses into useful, creative, and gratifying activities. But there will aways remain an irreducible minimum of tension which will find no such outlet. This will plague him, disturb him, and be responsible not only for his dreams but for many of his symptoms.

It is here that Cannon's pioneer work gave unintentional support to the argument. He began with his early studies on the movements of the intestines. By the use of x-ray he noticed that the orderly, rhythmic peristalsis stopped when the experimental animal was in a state of excitement. This simple observation opened up for him the whole field of bodily response to strong emotion. From it followed logically his studies on the emergency function of the adrenal glands. Thence he turned to a consideration of the sympathetic and autonomic nervous system. He provided us with knowledge of the anatomical pathways and physiological mechanisms through which strong emotions discharge and produce profound changes in the effector organs: for example, in the skin, the blood, the heart, the arteries, the muscles, the stomach and intestines, the bronchial tree, etc.

If a dog barks at a cat, the cat will arch its back, stiffen its legs, bare its teeth, and spit. Its pupils will dilate, and the hair will stand up on its back. Any dog can see that, and so can we. But Cannon saw more. He saw the blood pressure rise, the heart accelerate, the stomach and intestines stop contracting. He saw that there was a change in the blood distribution, that more of the blood left the peripheral parts of the body and concentrated in the vital organs, that the blood became enriched in glucose—carrying this readily available fuel to the muscles—and that the clotting time of the blood was shortened, so that a wound inflicted on such a frightened cat would not bleed so profusely as it would if the cat were in a state of purring contentment. He put all these findings together and explained them on the basis of an outpouring of adrenin—the secretion of the adrenal glands. He proved by a nice experiment that an increased production of adrenin actually occurred under circumstances of pain, hunger, fear, and rage. And he concluded that an animal in such a state of excitation was physiologically prepared for "fight or flight."

You will see that Cannon, Pavlov, and Freud were not far apart in their thinking, after all. Many of us go through life with our backs arched and our teeth bared—even when no one is barking at us. Perhaps we are conditioned to such a stance by events—real or imagined—of our childhood, to which we continue to react as if to an ever present memory. Such early experiences, especially when forgotten, can dog our footsteps throughout our lives. A slight stimulus later in life can then set off a train of responses having no realistic or adaptive purpose. Such responses may appear as symptoms of illness—perhaps as a headache or pain in the region of the heart or an attack of asthma or again as gastrointestinal disturbances.

Behind these symptoms one must search for an emotion or a set of emotions which serves as the detonator of a kind of chain reaction. It is the task of psychosomatic medicine to uncover such emotional tensions, to de-condition and re-educate the patient, in order to open up more useful and less destructive pathways to him. This is a new departure in medicine, although, of course, it relinquishes none of the established methods of medical treatment. It requires a training and understanding which most physicians and surgeons do not yet possess.

Take, for example, the puzzling problem of stomach ulcer. The psychological study of the lives of patients suffering from ulcer has brought important facts about them to light. Apparently they are burdened by certain characteristic conflicts which they are unable to resolve. What appears outwardly to be a hard-driving, active, efficient go-getter proves actually to be a hungry, dependent man whose unsatisfied cravings for love he is unable to accept because they are too humiliating to him. They do not correspond to the picture he has of himself. He tries hard to compensate for his essential weakness.

Indeed, he will often overcompensate. When his ambition is thwarted or his efforts toward success and accomplishment and leadership are too strained, he will have a tendency to run for cover, to slip back into a dependent childlike attitude, to put his thumb in his mouth, so to speak. Now there is reason to believe that these passive, receptive, thumb-sucking cravings, when not satisfied, as they can hardly be in such an upstanding he-man, and when continually repressed, find their expression in a primitive way. Just as anger and fear and pain may express themselves in the form of trembling and pallor and sweating, so the need to be loved and cared for, especially when denied, may express itself as a desire to be fed. The stomach is then constantly alerted and behaves as it does during digestion, continuously prepared for food that it does not receive.

This, in broad terms, is the formulation arrived at by Dr. Franz Alexander as the result of his psychoanalytic studies of a group of patients suffering from peptic ulcer. It represents, perhaps, only a rough approximation of the truth. No one has as yet conclusively demonstrated that a given emotional stimulus is inevitably and uniquely linked with a somatic disturbance. But Alexander's views are challenging and point the way for further investigations.

Dr. Harold Wolff, in his ingeniously conceived and carefully executed experiments, has borne out in the main the views of Alexander. These experiments were performed on his laboratory assistant, Tom—a modern Alexis St. Martin. Like his famous scientific progenitor William Beaumont, Dr. Wolff observed the stomach through an opening in the abdominal wall. This opening, or stoma, was produced surgically in Tom after accidental closure of his esophagus caused by drinking hot clam chowder. Dr. Wolff found that, when Tom's hostility or resentment or anxiety was aroused, the lining of his stomach became engorged and red, just as would his face; but when he was frightened or startled, both would pale. When the mucous lining of the stomach is in an engorged state, there is a sharp increase of acid production and vigorous muscular contraction of the stomach wall, and it is then unusually susceptible to injury. Even the most trifling damage results in hemorrhages and small erosions. If such an eroded area is deprived of its protective coating of mucus, an ulcer will form. Dr. Wolff was able to produce ulcers in Tom's stomach, but when covered with a protective dressing they quickly healed.

Interesting though they are, these observations are not astonishing. Today most internists are aware of the importance of emotional tension in the symptoms of patients suffering from ulcer and in their response to treatment. Indeed, a strange situation is arising in medical practice when patients of this kind are referred to psychiatrists for consultation. I saw one such recently. He was fidgety and ill at ease. At the close of the interview he said, "Gee, I didn't know it was going to be like this. I thought you would hypnotize me or give me one of those new drugs and get me to tell you something horrible about myself!" Actually, we had discussed his habits of life, his family situation, and his work. He was one of those eager, industrious men, always in a hurry, always too early for appointments, never satisfied with himself, a hard player, and a poor loser. I think one can say of such a person not that he complains of his stomach but that his stomach really complains of him. Perhaps the two can be helped to live together on better terms.

I have dealt with the problem of ulcer simply as an example because some of the best work in psychosomatic medicine has been done in this field. Actually, a psychosomatic approach can be legitimately and profitably applied to any illness, even a so-called "organic" one. It carries with it no exclusive imputation of "psychogenesis."

It has been so applied to asthma, to allergic reactions, to arterial hypertension, to coronary thrombosis, to diabetes, to the eczemas, to endocrine disturbances, to rheumatoid arthritis, to tuberculosis, and to many other illnesses. Even the occurrence of fractures and the tendency to suffer "accidents" was shown by Dunbar to be greatly influenced by inner psychological determinants. An example of this tendency was presented in the previous chapter—the case of the young paratrooper. In none of these disorders does this new point of view pretend to solve single-handed the problem of etiology. It concerns itself, moreover, with the effects of bodily states, such as organic illnesses and deformities, on the mental and emotional life as much as it does with the reverse. Since the war psychosomatic medicine has had much to do with the problems of adjustment presented by amputees, including the puzzling ones associated with "phantom limb." Indeed, the war (and its effects on servicemen and their families) has brought abundantly to our minds the fact that deeply repressed and unconscious conflicts—especially those centering in fear and hatred—are responsible for much mental as well as physical suffering.

Resistance to this idea has rapidly receded both among the sufferers themselves and among the younger generation of physicians. Even the old guard has had to give way before the avalanche of facts. New knowledge brings new problems. Psychosomatic medicine is not, however, a new specialty—but rather an old point of view revivified and enriched by new knowledge. As a springboard for research it will increase our understanding, and this in turn will enhance our skill in diagnosis and treatment. We are faced with the pressing need for postgraduate medical education in psychiatry and perhaps for a revision of our undergraduate curriculums. To the solution of these problems the leaders of medical education are now addressing themselves.

CHAPTER III

The Mind and the Heart

WHEN my former teacher, the late Dr. Richard Cabot, retired from the faculty of the Harvard Medical School to become professor of social ethics at Harvard College, he told me that he was going to keep his office on Marlborough Street for one purpose only and that was to reassure patients who had been informed by their private physicians that they had heart disease. He felt very strongly about the harm that many doctors unwittingly do by making a diagnosis of heart disease in the absence of sufficient evidence. Since those days, which corresponded to the end of World War I, we have learned a good deal about many aspects of cardiac disorders, especially about the coronary arteries and the nutrition of the heart muscle. Our knowledge is still insufficient. We often cannot be certain whether or not the heart is structurally damaged. In the absence of such knowledge it is natural for us to be cautious. We need to protect not only our patients but, quite justifiably, our own professional reputations. If we warn a man never to run upstairs, never to walk into a strong wind, never to lose his temper, we may, to be sure, be protecting his coronary system from one standpoint, although we may be hurting it from another. I do not in the least mean to imply that we should not warn him so, but if we do, we are also almost certainly arousing anxiety in him; and unless we protect him, as well as his heart muscle, against insults, we are falling short of our obligations.

I need hardly state that a large number of patients who

consult their doctors because of complaints centering in the heart do not have heart disease; nor need I tell you that the mention of heart disease terrifies most laymen. It is part of our daily work to make differential diagnoses between symptoms resulting from structural alteration of the heart and those due to anxiety. It is well known that these two states often coexist—that anxiety and tension may increase breathlessness and lower the threshold of pain and of visceral sensations, just as pain and breathlessness may give rise to anxiety and tension. The recent studies of Dr. Harold Wolff and his associates have shown us what we have all suspected, that even the rather trivial emotional disturbances of daily life alter the heart's function, raise the blood pressure and the cardiac rate, increase the stroke volume, and, in general, decrease the circulatory efficiency of the heart.

Perhaps it should be pointed out that the symptoms of structural heart disease are remarkably constant from patient to patient. Once these symptoms have been mastered, it is pretty safe to say that the other symptoms present are due not to heart disease but to other causes. An accurate assessment of symptoms is often the best means of differentiating between structural damage and cardiac disorders due to emotional disturbance. Such a differentiation is essential to intelligent handling of the cardiac patient because the treatment in the two conditions may be quite opposed. But one must bear in mind that the patient with structural damage to his heart is himself often anxious and emotionally disturbed, and many of his complaints may be the result of this disturbance rather than of his cardiac lesion.

Pain and breathlessness are cardinal symptoms of heart damage, but they are both often present in the so-called "cardiac neuroses." What can one say about the difference in character of these manifestations in the two states?

Anginal pain, no matter where radiated, characteristically occurs in the mid-sternal line. Cardiac pain associated with anxiety or tension is much more likely to occur over the apex. Unless a neurotic patient has been briefed by witnessing a true anginal attack, he will very rarely complain of mid-line pain. Anginal pain characteristically lasts from one to two minutes and is very quickly relieved by nitroglycerine. Pain associated with anxiety or tension often lasts much longer, and, although it may be relieved by nitroglycerine, relief is slower in coming. The patient with true angina usually knows what brought on the attack of pain, whether it be due to exercise or excitement, and he will immediately stop doing the thing that caused his discomfort. The other patient usually does not know how to account for his pain, which may come on at any time, even while resting comfortably and while apparently relaxed. Furthermore, the patient with true angina has great difficulty in describing the quality of his pain, while the other patient elaborates too willingly on it.

There are analogous differences in the dyspnea experienced by the patient with structural heart disease and by the patient without. The first is more likely to have panting respirations, the second more likely to feel as if he could not take a deep breath. Again, orthopnea is more common in the first than in the second.

Other differences could be enumerated. But these facts are widely known to enlightened internists. If that is so, what, then, has psychiatry to offer further to this subject? I think that it has a not inconsiderable contribution to make to the management and therapy of patients suffering from disorders of the heart.

I should like to discuss, therefore, some of the psychological phenomena seen in cardiac patients. Since this subject is a large one, we shall make better headway by restricting the discussion to three aspects of the problem.

These three aspects will also coincide roughly with three age groups. The first group consists of children and young people who suffer from various forms of rheumatic heart disease. The second group consists of people of early and middle age who suffer from so-called "cardiac neuroses," and the third group, which I shall deal with only briefly, consists of people of middle and late middle life who suffer from coronary insufficiency and coronary occlusion. This division into age groups is, of course, somewhat arbitrary, but, even if not wholly accurate, it will serve our purpose best if we permit it to stand.

Concerning the first group, composed of youthful, rheumatic cardiac invalids, I think that it is probably accurate to say that their psychological difficulties are, in general, subject to several important variables (omitting for the moment the personal characteristics of the patients themselves): One is the severity of the cardiac disability; another is its duration; and still another is the nature of the medical management to which these patients are subjected and, perhaps most important of all, the attitude which their parents take toward them and their illness. Whether these patients are seriously disabled or not, certain psychological difficulties invariably arise, especially so if the illness confines them to inactivity or to close supervision for any protracted period.

Let us now consider the nature of these problems: What psychological phenomena are we likely to find? Are they confined to the patient himself? What implications can be gleaned from them as to therapeutic management?

Here is a case in point:

Johnny is the eldest child of three. He is just thirteen; a skinny, lanky, active, intelligent, good-humored boy. He is well liked at school and is a reasonably good student and is very keen on basketball and wrestling. He plays forward on the junior high school basketball team. He has been no special trouble to his parents, and, except for an extremely disorderly room and a great disinclination to wash and bathe, they seldom have to correct him. But he has not gained weight and often seems listless and tired and has looked pale and has had dark circles under his eyes. In addition, he has complained of vague pains in his legs and recently has had one or two nosebleeds. All this has caused his mother some concern.

One evening he complained of headache and felt feverish. He had no appetite. He slept poorly; and, when his mother went in to see him, he complained that his legs ached. The next morning she sent for their pediatrician. There seemed no doubt at all about the diagnosis. Johnny's mother, who was well posted in medical matters, said after they had left the room: "What about his heart, Doctor? I saw you listening to it for a long time." The doctor said: "He has a slightly suspicious murmur; we'll have to watch it and keep him perfectly still for the present." That was easy because Johnny felt too wretched to do anything but lie quietly in bed and take the medicine given him. In a week's time he was a good deal better. But the doctor continued to come every day and always listened carefully to the boy's heart. Johnny was fascinated with the electrocardiogram, and the doctor explained all about it to him. His mother stood at the bedside with her eyes glued on the doctor's face. She was always cheerful and controlled, but naturally she was terribly worried. The doctor explained to her that, although the valvular damage might be slight, what counted was the heart muscle, which needed protection while the process was active; that Johnny would have to stay in bed until there were no signs of activity; and that when he returned to school, he would still have to be careful. He added: "I guess there'll be no basketball this year." His mother knew that would be the greatest blow of all, but she counted on the boy's sense and co-operative spirit.

This story has a happy ending. The boy made a good recovery. But you can see that he was fortunate. He had a careful doctor, an intelligent and understanding mother, and he himself was sufficiently alert so that his energies could be diverted into channels other than basketball and wrestling. Partly through the interest which the electrocardiogram had awakened in him he set to work to assemble a very respectable radio.

If we vary any of the ingredients of this story, we might have quite a different situation on our hands. A less biddable youth than Johnny, for example, a somewhat unruly, defiant, rowdy adolescent at loggerheads with his parents, may present a trying therapeutic challenge. This is especially true if the child feels the restrictions of his illness to be a kind of punishment or if the parents ease their own concern and hostility by exploiting the situation and threatening the child. Even trained nurses have been known to say to such children: "If you don't keep quiet, the doctor says you're liable to drop dead of heart failure."

From a psychological point of view there are two principal problems to deal with: One is in the patient; the other is in his parents. The chief problem in the child is to prevent boredom and to still the restlessness which so quickly overtakes him when he is deprived of his accustomed bodily activities and finally to teach him what he can and cannot do, depending on the amount of cardiac damage. Early in his illness the child can be lifted from his bed into a comfortable steamer chair. Such a change in posture puts no extra strain on his heart but, on the other hand, may improve his morale greatly.

Soon after the acute toxic symptoms have subsided, the

services of a visiting teacher are essential. The longer the child is sick, the more necessary this becomes, not so much to prevent loss of schooling as to provide some interest and substitutive activity and to prevent his slipping into a regressed, withdrawn state in which his chief satisfactions are in daydreaming. If lessons can be combined with, or supplemented by, interesting occupational therapy, so much the better.

The problem of the parent is the more difficult to deal with and the more important. The bugaboo of rheumatic fever is the ever present danger of recurring attacks with further damage to the heart. It is difficult to instruct a mother to be on the lookout for vague symptoms of reinfection, which are the common ones in childhood, without arousing undue anxiety in her and eventually, by contagion, in her child. If we do arouse too much anxiety, then she will overprotect her child, worry over him, fuss over him, keep him in bed long hours, urge him to eat, and be alarmed at the slightest headache or evidence of fatigue. It is easy to guess how a spirited child or a compliant one will react to such treatment. Or, again, an overanxious mother may, because of her fear, be blind to fairly obvious signs of trouble and assume a casual attitude which may be even more damaging than the oversolicitous one.

I have no magic formula to apply to this puzzling problem. But this much I can say: If the doctor aims to provide an atmosphere in which recovery from the first attack is facilitated and recurrences are to be prevented, then he must address himself to the concerns, to the worries, and to the emotions of the mother. It is probably as important to listen to her as it is to listen to the patient's heart.

Although I have emphasized the place of the child's mother in all this, the attitude of physicians, of nurses and attendants—whether in a teaching hospital, an outpatient department, or a cardiac home—is often of determining importance. If the child is to recover from the body blow that nature has dealt him and is to regain a place in his world, no matter how handicapped, then he must be taught the two most difficult lessons of childhood, if not of life: one is to defer an immediate satisfaction for an ultimate gain; the other is to accept certain inexorable limitations of his capacities. He will learn these lessons best if those responsible for him are themselves not overburdened with anxiety. We should not, of course, fail to recognize the anxieties that the child himself is coping with. These may be mobilized and aggravated by the illness, though by no means solely caused by it.

Throughout this chapter you will find the word "anxiety" frequently used. It is the most important psychological manifestation in cardiac patients. In the group I have just discussed, anxiety is more to be reckoned with in the parent than in the sick person. In the next group, sufferers from what are called "cardiac neuroses," anxiety is of cardinal importance in the patient himself and in the formation of his symptoms. The term "cardiac neurosis" is a loose one. It is a diagnostic catchall to define those patients who have unpleasant, often frightening, sensations which they attribute to their hearts or, again, who exhibit what we like to call functional disturbances of their hearts, such as tachycardia, palpitations, and even sometimes extra-systoles.

When a consultant examines such a patient and uses the most modern scientific equipment and after great care can find no evidence of structural damage to the cardiovascular system, then the patient, if he has the temerity and extravagance to cling to his symptoms, is said to be suffering from a "cardiac neurosis."

Within the past few years it has become increasingly customary to send such a patient to a psychiatrist. When he arrives (let us call him Jones), the first thing he will talk about is the fact that he is in a psychiatrist's office. He is a bit shamefaced about that. He says that he has never done such a thing before—as if he had been caught stealing money from his grandmother. This is an old story to the psychiatrist, who soon puts his patient at ease. The next thing that comes up is the fact that Jones thinks that the doctor thinks that all his symptoms are imaginary; otherwise he would not have been sent to see a psychiatrist. This, too, is disposed of by the psychiatrist's reassuring and sympathetic attention. He explains to Jones that no symptoms are imaginary, if they are actually experienced, and that no one ever suspected him of malingering. The rest of the hour then is spent on a list of complaints and symptoms.

The psychiatrist pays close attention to the way in which the patient tells his story. He does not ask him too many questions in the first visit. What he is trying to do is to make a diagnosis—a psychiatric diagnosis—because on that will depend the choice of treatment and, in part, the prognosis.

Jones I is a man in the early fifties. For the past few days he has felt strangely apprehensive. He is tremulous, and his hands are cold and moist. He says that he has been having dizzy spells. On closer inquiry he does not actually experience vertigo but momentary states of confusion with feelings of breathlessness and oppression in the region of the diaphragm. He has had difficulties before for which he has consulted a neurologist, and he is accustomed to a certain degree of tension and apprehensiveness. This time, however, it is much more intense and disturbing. He feels panicky and convinced that there is something seriously wrong with his heart.

What happened was this: A year ago he was examined by his company physician, an excellent and well-trained young internist. This internist noticed in the electrocardiogram evidence of a wide S bundle branch block that had been present, according to previous electrocardiographic evidence obtained, over a period of two years. He said nothing to the patient about it, assuring him that everything was normal. A year later a new company physician re-examined him and told him that there was something unusual in his E.K.G. This disturbed the patient greatly; and, since the two company doctors had not agreed, he consulted a cardiologist. The cardiologist examined him carefully and made light of the finding, explaining it to him (at least so the patient told me) as a "slight surge of the S wave." This, of course, meant nothing to the patient, and, let me add, it meant equally little to me. The only difference was that it was the patient's heart and not mine, so it did not frighten me as it did him. I inquired as to the real meaning of the electrocardiographic changes and then took great pains to explain things to the patient and to reassure him. He was much relieved to discover that he was suffering only from his old familiar neurotic difficulties, and he was able then and there to give up his heart disease. This was a gratifying, if superficial, result. The man leads an active, useful, and full life, and there seemed at that time no justification for exploring further into his emotional problems. It is by no means always so easy to lay a cardiac ghost as it was in this case of anxiety neurosis.

Take Jones II for example: He is thirty years old, an extremely intelligent statistician. He was sent to me by an excellent cardiologist because the patient could not be convinced that there was nothing seriously wrong with his heart. He complained of palpitations at night. He would awaken with his heart pounding. He had vague pains throughout his chest. He said that at college he got too much exercise and had "sprung his heart." He said that he was conscious of his "heart beating all around the bush." He said: "I was scared into a perfect jelly and thought of taking up religion to die a good Christian death." He was told not to dance, and he began to be very careful of his health. He had many other bodily preoccupations and spent hours every day brooding over his aches and pains and over his damaged heart. He had a bizarre and extravagant way of describing his feelings. He compared himself to "an old tooth waiting to be filled" and said that he felt as if his heart were "rotting."

The manner in which he presented his complaints, the semijesting, jocular, inappropriate affect which accompanied his bizarre and disturbing thoughts, as well as his fixed hypochondriacal preoccupations, convinced me that this was a seriously disturbed man with certain features of his makeup characteristic of schizophrenia. This diagnosis was supported by psychological tests made by another examiner, who described the patient accurately as an "intellectually compensated latent schizophrenic."

In a patient of this sort there is no use in attempting to approach the cardiac complaint directly. It has all the fixity and stubbornness of certain paranoid delusions. One can reassure him from time to time, but reassurances do not stick. The wisest course is to disregard the symptoms and to address one's self to the whole life-situation and to try to keep the patient in contact with others and with reality. This man had a brilliant military record, achieving high rank. His gifted scientific mind was put to excellent use.

Jones III presents quite a different picture, different diagnosis, different treatment, and different outlook. In November, 1945, I received a letter from Dr. Blank, who wrote: "I am referring Mr. L. W. K. to you for your valued opinion and care. He is a high-strung man with hypochondriacal symptoms and a labile hypertension." There was inclosed in the letter an abstract of the history and physical findings. The important facts were these: He was thirty-six years old; his blood pressure in the right arm was 180/100; in the right leg, 190/105. The patient had been hospitalized and given intravenous sodium amytal. After injection of this drug his blood pressure fell to 140/82. The heart was apparently normal, and renal functional tests were within normal limits. An intravenous pyelogram showed slight distention of the kidney pelves. The diagnosis was "essential hypertension with a very prominent nervous factor in its origin."

This patient came willingly for psychiatric help. He was very much frightened–frightened that he would be permanently invalided because of his hypertension. He saw himself in a wheelchair after a stroke. He feared a sudden heart attack or that he might have to undergo a sympathectomy. He had many of the symptoms common in hypertensives: headache, buzzing in the ears, occasional precordial oppression, and heaviness in the left arm. Further inquiry revealed a long history of neurotic complaints. He said of himself that he had always been overconcerned with his health. For a long time his gastrointestinal tract was the chief focus of his discomfort and concern, but his anxiety had now attached itself to his blood pressure.

In spite of his disabilities he was an able and effective young business executive. His father, too, suffered from hypertension. I concluded that everything should be done to prevent this man's still labile blood pressure from becoming fixed at a high level. After further preliminary psychological studies I recommended psychoanalysis.

Two years after receiving the letter from the referring physician I wrote him the following letter:

DEAR DR. BLANK:

Mr. L. W. K. had his last session on November 6. As you know, he has had to be away a good deal on business trips. He has just returned from one to the West without his usual emotional and physiological upsets. This trip required his making several speeches, which he was able to do without stage fright or cold sweats. His family doctor took his blood pressure about two weeks ago and found it to be 120/70. I think that he has finally abandoned a conviction that he has hypertension, but he is still very gun shy of the blood pressure cuff. I imagine that he always will be.

Let me review briefly what transpired during the psychoanalytical treatment. As is usual in such treatment, one begins with the immediate and disturbing facts of the patient's life—the ones which he naturally first chooses to talk about. In this case it was his health and his worries over his future and the support of his family. What would happen to them if he should become permanently invalided? Gradually we penetrated behind this outer coating of defense and found in him a frightened, puny, pimply youth whose father had walked out on his mother. His father had had terrible rages, and yet he was to the son the ideal of a strong and heroic figure whom he remembered as an officer in World War I. But the father never came back to them. The boy was left alone with an adoring, but bitter and unhappy, mother. They lived in a part of the States where to be divorced was a permanent disgrace for a woman. The patient felt this keenly, became prematurely ambitious and self-reliant. He led his class at school but remained physically weak. He looked admiringly and enviously at the football stalwarts. This notion of weakness clung to him, and in spite of more than usual success in his professional and domestic life it seemed to load the dice against him. Behind his driving ambition there was great insecurity, great lack of self-confidence. What he actually wanted was failure and illness and to be taken care of. It was the old story of an unconscious wish being experienced as a conscious fear. All this was revealed to the patient, not as an intellectual process, but as a personal experience through which he passed gradually, accompanied by many disturbing emotions. Although the end result seems favorable, time alone will tell whether what he gained will remain with him permanently.

I have presented this patient as another example of an anxiety neurosis. He resembles the first one, the man who was so frightened because of his S wave, and the second one, who was afflicted with hypochondriacal preoccupations. And yet the treatment in all three was different and in each case was aimed at the life-situation and personality rather than at the cardiovascular symptoms.

There are many patients who exhibit far less *overt* anxiety than these three did. For example, I have in mind a woman of thirty-eight whose history was one of tachycardia for a period of about fifteen years. Her basic heart rate was usually 130–140 per minute, at times reaching a level of over 200. At other times, however, her rate dropped to 90 or even 80 to the minute. She had consulted a great many doctors (some very distinguished ones), and her list of medicines included atropine, digitalis, mecholyl, phenobarbital, and quinidine. She had also had pressure exerted on her eyeballs, vagi, and carotid sinuses, all without relief. And yet the heart was perfectly normal to examination, Nothing was ever found but paroxysmal auricular tachycardia.

She was repeatedly advised to have psychiatric consultation. She admitted having had a "nervous breakdown" before the trouble began, but she said that she was quite able to analyze her own emotional difficulties and that she saw no necessity whatever for psychotherapy. She had rejected all conceivable reasons for being nervous or tense.

In a patient of this sort it is sometimes impossible to proceed psychiatrically. The whole emotional conflict is in a sense acted out by the heart. This is a true organ neurosis. Her unconscious drives are so threatening to her that they cannot reach the level of consciousness. They appear to find escape through a specific visceral disorder. And yet, psychological tests made on this patient showed a neurotic disturbance reaching serious proportions.

It would take us a little too far afield to discuss how we arrive at our diagnostic formulations in these patients. Among other things, we take into account their attitude toward the disorder, whether symptoms are diffuse or circumscribed, the type of sense organ that is involved, and whether the symptoms are subjective only or observable by others.

Usually in these so-called "cardiac neuroses" we have to differentiate between hypochondriasis, anxiety neuroses, and organ neuroses, and sometimes hysteria, in its technical, not its popular, sense. None is necessarily exclusive of the others, but the indications for treatment may depend upon the weighting of these various components. In all of them anxiety plays the predominant dynamic role. I will not attempt to define anxiety now but defer that to a later chapter. Let me emphasize only that it is not entirely equivalent to fear and legitimate worry. It is a complicated emotional state in which hostility or rage as a defense against fear is also mobilized. There are unconscious elements in anxiety that explain why it is not always accessible to a rational common-sense approach, why the accompanying cardiac symptoms of anxiety so often persist in spite of our best efforts at reassurance. In any case, we need to know what to reassure about.

The psychiatrist must make up his mind whether to explore and to uncover the deeper sources of anxiety or whether to help his patient cover them up and work out some compromise with the aid of repression. The choice will depend upon the age, adaptability, intelligence, and strength of character of the patient and on his capacity and willingness to relinquish symptoms.

In the older age group, about which I will say a few words now, effective psychotherapy is by no means ruled out, but it is often difficult, especially in the presence of extensive cerebral arteriosclerosis. The group I have in mind are the sufferers from anginal attacks, from coronary insufficiency and infarction, and from beginning symptoms of failure. Even though these patients have outspoken structural damage to their hearts, one must not conclude that emotional influences play no role in their illness or in their recovery.

Any experienced clinician can cull from his memory instances in which a profound emotional upset was followed by what we call a coronary accident.

A former president of the New York Heart Association recently told me of two such episodes in his clinical experience. The first concerned a man who heard the screeching of brakes and the crash of automobiles in front of his house. He dashed to the window only to see his own son's car in the wreck; whereupon he was seized with gripping substernal pain characteristic of a coronary occlusion.

The second story was about an elderly physician with hypertension. He began to complain of slight indigestion and, being somewhat hypochondriacal, he feared at once that he had a cancer of the stomach. But he did not seek medical advice. Instead he brooded over his illness and said to himself: "If I have lost weight, then I surely have a cancer." After days of torturesome worry he finally summoned up enough courage to step upon the scales; but before it registered, he suffered a sudden coronary occlusion and died shortly thereafter.

Such histories could be multiplied out of any physician's experiences, I am sure. Perhaps it is wise to draw no etiological inferences from them, to recognize them as remarkable coincidences, and to realize that coincidences are themselves facts of nature which merit study. We do know that outbursts of rage or startle reactions, as from fright or the hearing of bad news, are sometimes followed by sudden cardiac deaths.

We have less information about the influence of prolonged anxiety or states of tension on the coronary circulation. On this matter our suspicions are not yet based on proved physiological observations. Inferences may, however, be drawn from illuminating observations, many of them emanating from Harold Wolff's laboratory, on the peripheral and visceral circulation. The vascular supply to the mucous membrane of the stomach (and also of the nose) alters with the emotional state of the subject: rage appears to be accompanied by engorgement of the lining of the stomach and sudden fear by blanching. Analogous changes occur in the bladder, the vagina, and the large bowel. From Mittelmann's experiments we have learned that finger temperature may drop as many as 25° F. when the subject is in a state of anxiety. And, again, Homer Smith's studies have demonstrated a reduction in renal blood flow up to 40 per cent under similar conditions.

The two original experiments of Homer Smith have been corroborated and extended by Pfeiffer, working in Wolff's laboratory. In eighteen patients suffering from arterial hypertension, rises in both systolic and diastolic pressures were observed when relevant life-situations were touched upon in interviews with them. Accompanying these rises in pressure, there was a renal vasoconstriction reflected by decreases in the renal plasma flow up to 25 per cent of the control levels. This sometimes outlasted the rise in systemic blood pressure. In some cases the peripheral resistance to renal blood flow increased by as much as 40 per cent. Wolff and Pfeiffer conclude that the kidney, in persons with arterial hypertension, exhibits an abnormal vascular pattern characterized by increased arteriolar tone which is further increased by threats or assaults to the organism—physical or psychological. Such vasoconstriction, if prolonged, may damage the kidney parenchyma and eventually the brain and the heart. These conclusions support the theoretical ones proposed by others and myself in a monograph on the personality in arterial hypertension.

Finally, let me add that there is evidence in the literature that cardiac pain occurring under circumstances of emotional stress is associated with electrocardiographic changes. Artificially produced extra-cardiac pain may be associated with similar changes. Whether these are the result of a diminished blood supply to the heart muscle because of vasoconstriction or are due to an extra demand for oxygen because of increased work is not yet clear.

Aside from considerations of etiology, however, sound therapy will have to take into account the patient's emotional state. There are some for whom prolonged bed rest acts as an irritant and whom sedatives will not quiet unless they are given adequate psychotherapy. According to some recent observations similar preparation is necessary in some patients before digitalis can be effective.

It is my impression that almost everyone who suffers an infarction goes through a period of depression, sometimes quite severe. It may long outlast electrocardiographic evidences of damage to the heart and may delay restoration to even moderate functioning. But these depressed states usually yield in time to the faithful ministrations of the physician and especially to a regime of gradually increasing activity. They do not often require the special services of a psychiatrist. There is no better psychotherapy for the cardiac invalid than to be permitted and encouraged to exercise when such advice is compatible with his cardiac reserve.

The heart and the precordial area are quickly responsive to emotional stimuli, and, reciprocally, sensations coming from these structures are often felt and interpreted as emotions. The Greeks, you will recall, looked upon the midriff as the seat of the soul and not only as an aphrodisiac to which one applies suntan oil.

Perhaps the poets could write for us a real treatise on the irregularities of the heart, that extraordinarily acrobatic and versatile organ which leaps and bounds and jumps and turns over and sinks and rises and catches fire and freezes and is light as a feather or as heavy as lead. Finally it stops; and that is what we are all afraid of.

CHAPTER IV

Psychotherapy in Arterial Hypertension

In considering the complicated subject of arterial hypertension it is appropriate at this time to review the experiences with psychotherapy. Both in this approach and in others there is admittedly a great deal that we do not yet know. Professor George Santayana used to talk about defining the limits of our ignorance. What are these limits?

We do not know, for example, whether the process is a reversible one, whether the impulses which give rise to arteriolar constriction are humoral or neural in origin, or both. In spite of the brilliant researches of Goldblatt and others, we do not know what part the kidneys and the renal circulation play in bringing it about. Indeed, it would be hard for us to define this disease further than to say that it represents a morbid state in which elevation of the systolic and diastolic blood pressures—either fluctuating or constant—occurs in association with arteriolar vasoconstriction. We do not know why the life-expectancy of some is unaffected, while others succumb quickly to the malignant form.

Once we thought that hypertension was associated with a certain bodily habitus—that it was more prone to exist among the short and the squat and the red-faced. Those who have occasion to see patients suffering from this disturbance have found them to be lean and spare, tall and pale-faced as well. According to Page, "an accurate correlation of body build, height and surface area with arterial pressure cannot be established." Again citing Page as my authority, and contrary to generally accepted beliefs, there is no sufficiently documented testimony to support the view that heredity plays a vital part in the origin of hypertension. He cautions against ascribing too great importance to heredity and suggests that this aspect of the problem needs reinvestigation on a more comprehensive basis.

This, then, is part of the staked-out claim of our ignorance. To outline it is not to underestimate the importance of recent researches and their contribution to our understanding of the physiological mechanisms of this disorder.

That it has still another aspect is now rather generally accepted. In this terrain our ignorance is even wider and more varied. It would be a challenge, indeed, to plumb its depths and to chart its perimeter. I am speaking now, of course, of the psychological aspects of arterial hypertension which some have attempted to explore: Alexander, Menninger, Moschowitz, Rennie, Saul, and Weiss among others. In collaboration with others, I have myself put in four years at hard labor breaking ground. I cannot say that we struck gold, but I hope at least that we uncovered some facts. This investigation was based on the clinical and psychiatric study of twenty-four patients suffering from arterial hypertension.

I should like to say here that the description of the personalities of these patients which I shall presently offer and which derives from our own work and, in part, from that of others does not, in all probability, apply uniquely or exclusively to the hypertensive state, though none of our patients differed widely from it. I have, myself, yet to be convinced that characterological studies made by those interested in psychosomatic medicine have any specific etiological significance. Not beauty alone but artifacts as well may dwell in the eye of the beholder.

The facts that appear from our own studies and from others' are these: Sufferers from arterial hypertension exhibit a disorder of personality which has been conveniently described by the term "neurotic." This disorder manifests itself in their interpersonal relationships, in their sexual adjustments, and often in their occupational achievements. They are characteristically tense individuals given to states of anxiety and depression. Much of their emotional tension can be ascribed to inhibited, but not deeply repressed, aggressive impulses. It is often possible to trace the history of this neurotic development of character to early childhood when the common feature is an extreme degree of insecurity, with a greatly unsatisfied dependent relationship to a threatening parent. Given this bad start, the patient then falters through life—unable to relax, unable to enter into secure and satisfying relationships, always on the defensive, ready to fight but afraid to fight.

With this precarious adjustment the applecart of the patient's emotions is easily upset. The death of a parent or of a partner, a motor accident, the illness of a child, business reverses—almost any event which jeopardizes his security, which is felt either directly or by implication as a threat to his life, increases to an intolerable degree the quantum of his anxiety and of his reactive depression. In our series of cases it was observed that the clinical discovery of elevated blood pressure frequently coincided with such a traumatic experience.

I do not wish to be understood as stating that this disturbance of character or its ultimate outcome is the cause of hypertension. It is, on the contrary, my suspicion that the psychological disorder and the physiological disorder each represents a different aspect of a more basic disturbance, the nature and cause of which is unknown—though its existence is often foreshadowed early in life.

What therapeutic implications are to be drawn from these observed facts and from this theoretical interpretation of them? The first is that psychotherapy cannot be directed at blood vessels. It can be directed at the emotions. Its aim is to treat the person, not the vasoconstrictor mechanism. This must be kept clearly in mind. What we can accomplish will depend, as in any other therapeutic procedure, not only upon our skill but also upon the material with which we are forced to deal. It is not a plastic, easily workable one. These patients have usually extraordinarily rigid personalities. Their aggressions are fixed; they are not fluid or readily mobilizable. If they were, these patients would have spontaneously found a more satisfactory and less destructive expression for them. Much of their anxiety is absorbed in their symptoms. It is not easily dislodged, and when it is, it may sweep over them and produce a state bordering on panic. The underlying depression is constantly being fed by the conviction that they are sufferers from a fell malady, that fate has dealt them a body blow. Each symptom winds up the mainspring of their tension, increases their anxiety, and undoubtedly reflects itself in their vascular apparatus. Deep psychotherapy in this illness is, therefore, no task for the bungler or the amateur. It is as dangerous, as delicate, and as difficult as surgery.

Like the surgeon the psychotherapist must know something of the topographical anatomy of his patient. His aims are to restore a more normal functioning of the emotions. Persuasion and reassurance, though important tools, are seldom sufficient. They will not remove tough bands of connective tissue, and they will seldom remove the strictures and inhibitions against which these patients live their unfulfilled lives.

Again like surgery, the choice of procedure will depend not upon preconceived doctrinaire generalizations but upon careful clinical observation. It is as absurd to say that every patient suffering from hypertension should undergo psychoanalysis as it is to say that every case of neoplastic disease should be operated upon. The decision is based, first of all, upon the patient's ability to stand operation, second, upon the nature of the lesion and its accessibility, and, third, upon the prospects for a successful result. Surgeons no longer operate because there is nothing else to do but rather for specific reasons empirically derived. In the domain of psychiatry and psychoanalysis the same critical standards are now, happily, being invoked.

The surgeons have, to be sure, a great advantage over us; not only is their handiwork more precise, but their results are referable to a statistic which it would be folly to assert that we possess. We have none.

Lacking a statistic, we can, at best, proceed according to certain rational principles. I have stated what they are. The problem is that of treating a severe character neurosis in which anxiety, depression, and suppressed aggression are the cardinal psychopathological features. The method of choice will vary from cheerful neglect (based on that much-vaunted common sense which we are all supposed to possess in such good measure) to deep psychological exploration. The latter you will grant is a matter for the expert. What is to be hoped from it we cannot say. There is as yet no sufficient evidence that psychoanalysis or any other psychotherapeutic procedure can reverse the physiological process or change the destiny of this disease—be it benign or malignant. The problem is an open one. It needs further investigation. The ground has now been cleared for such an undertaking. It is probable that we can do more by way of prevention than of cure.

There is evidence that a correlation exists between levels of pressure and emotional disturbance and that suitable psychotherapy can ameliorate some symptoms, such as headache, fatigue, palpitation, dizziness, shortness of breath, and the fear which these engender.

We have observed this ourselves and so have others. Weiss has stated, for example: "For some time now I have felt and taught that essential hypertension cannot be eradicated by any psychotherapeutic process but that almost every patient can be benefitted by psychotherapy." In a review of the records of 200 consecutive patients with symptoms of hypertension he selected 144 which "seemed to correspond to the clinical picture of so-called essential hypertension" (note the cautious conservatism of his words). Ninety-three of these lent themselves to satisfactory psychosomatic investigation, and in only 7 did he conclude that psychic factors bore no relationship either to the onset of hypertension or to the production of symptoms. Case I of his series shows a quite remarkable coincidence between periods of elevated blood pressure and vasospastic retinitis with episodes that gave rise to anxiety and with what Weiss calls periods of "throttled aggression."

In Alexander's carefully studied psychoanalytic material he presents blood pressure readings of 161/110 when his patient was emotionally disturbed as compared with 142/98 when calm. Saul has made similar observations of fluctuations of blood pressure with mood and, more especially, with variations in the intensity of the so-called "transference" situation. It must be borne in mind, however, that fluctuations may occur spontaneously without reference to known therapeutic effects.

The most striking, unique, and dramatic case in the literature is a patient of Lewis B. Hill, who recalled early in the course of psychoanalytic treatment a deeply suppressed childhood memory. This was brought up with intense emotion. The patient exhibited an extraordinary degree of rage and guilt over a childhood experience in which his mother struck him with a pony whip. The recall and reliving of this traumatic episode was followed by a critical sustained and enduring fall of both systolic and diastolic pressures. Perhaps this single observation is a prototype of others to come. But, in honesty, it must be said that from a clinical and physiological point of view the case is insufficiently documented and the diagnosis remains open to question.

Now, leaving out of consideration all efforts at deeper psychodynamic inquiry and turning to the everyday handling of these patients, I believe that our new knowledge can be put to effective use. We are dealing with tender vessels. They need to be protected from emotional strain, especially from demands upon a self-reliance they do not possess. There is no good in telling them to "buck up" and "forget it." They need the maximum of reassurance about the disease itself. They need very much to feel that some one person is watching over them and will take on his shoulders the burdens of their worries. They need to be encouraged to express their aggression, not by hurling dishes or epithets at their wives, but by directed work and play and by physical exercise, if this is compatible with their cardiac reserve. They need to be weaned away from an overconcern with the level of their blood pressure. The experienced doctor will vary his methods. With some he will be frank, with others he will be silent, and with some he will have to dissemble. The manner in which this frightening fact is first presented to them is of the utmost significance. If the doctor shows his own alarm when the mercury column tops 220, it is likely to be communicated at once to his patients.

It is well to remember that almost all our therapy involves psychotherapy. Drugs and sedatives, rest and exercise, diet and baths, all have psychotherapeutic implications; and this is just as true of surgery. The surgical amphitheater has threatened to become the court of last resort in this illness. Perhaps in time we will learn on what findings nature bases her verdict—why some patients respond to sympathectomy with a reduction in blood pressure, a recession of retinitis, and a merciful relief from headache, while others do not. Perhaps the attitude which patients bring to the ordeal of operation may in some measure determine its effect upon them. For there are those who face it as they would doom, and there are others who look upon it as a deliverance.

CHAPTER V

What Can We Learn from a Medical History?

EXPERIENCE teaches most of us that time spent in taking a careful medical history is time well spent and will save wasted motions later. What we actually can learn will depend, of course, on our skill and on the patient's willingness and capacity to co-operate with us. Although I shall discuss later both of these topics, it will be more appropriate to consider first what we should aim at in taking a medical history.

Naturally this will depend on our purpose. As I understand it the purpose of taking a medical history is to record a series of events that have culminated in the illness or disorder for which the patient has consulted us. It is assumed that from such a record we shall get some understanding of the sick person and of his ailment and, furthermore, that others trained in medicine will derive a similar understanding from reading the history that we have written down.

No medical history, however, can reproduce accurately what occurs in nature. It is at best a kind of stylized symbolic representation of certain human experiences in much the same way that a map is a stylized symbolic representation of a landscape. The value of a good map will depend upon the accuracy of its scale and upon the picturing of the relationship of certain important land masses, contours, bodies of water, as well as certain man-made structures such as railroads and large settlements. With the aid of such a map we can find our way around in strange country. But if the map depicts every culvert, duck pond, and hot-dog stand and leaves out mountain ranges and navigable rivers, we will soon go astray if we rely upon it. Just so a good medical history will portray in the dimension of time, rather than of space, the influences, past and present, that are important in the development of the patient and his disorder. You may justifiably catch me up on the word "important." There is no question about the importance of a mountain range or a navigable river, but who is to say what is important in the record of a patient's life? If we depend wholly on his judgment, then of what use is our medical knowledge? And if we depend wholly on our own preconceived notions, then we will arrive at a kind of standardized history which includes everything and tells us nothing.

When I was an intern, we were brought up to take just such histories. We would approach a patient, and, after recording his complaint (this we were taught to put down strictly in the patient's own words, an excellent habit to which I have always clung), we would write the letters *F.H.* for family history. That was quickly disposed of. The patient's *F* was *l & w*, but his *M* had unfortunately *d* of typhoid fever. A number of *S*'s *&* *B*'s were usually *l & w*, or a couple might have *d* in infancy. And then the ritual was to say that the *F.H.* was otherwise "noncontributory" (a truly fabulous misconception!) and that there was no tuberculosis (later we added "or known exposure") or malignant disease in the family.

We would then go on to the *P.H.* No illness or accident would escape us. We were as persistent as a cigar-smoking detective in a movie melodrama and about as subtle. I recall asking a young woman about her weight. What was her present weight, her weight last year, her heaviest? When I asked her what her lightest weight was and she said "5½ lbs.," I began to get the notion that perhaps I was boring her by the third-degree method.

I recall the chief attending physician, a sober and pedestrian man, asking a little boy of eight whether the pain in his groin radiated to his penis and testicles. The child looked up bewildered and said "What's them?"

Then with a rumble of drums came the last and final act of the circus: the *P.I.* This was a new event, a thing in itself, a calamity, a misfortune, an act of God like a hurricane or an earthquake. It had little to do with past events and less with what today we call the personality.

Our histories were nothing if not complete. They covered pages of carefully written foolscap. The greatest sin was the sin of omission. And they bore about as much resemblance to the true story of the patient's life as a Mercator projection does to the contours of the earth's surface.

During World War I for a time I was put in charge of a large medical ward in a base hospital in France. Although I was only a first lieutenant, casual officers, outranking me by several grades, were assigned to this ward for instruction in physical diagnosis. One of them had the habit of turning in long and rambling medical histories that stretched out interminably and arrived nowhere. I urged this officer as tactfully as I could to stick to the essentials. The next history that he wrote up was a short one. It said:

> Complaint: Abdominal pain.
> Past history: Kicked by a steer.
> Diagnosis: Tonsillitis.

This has always seemed to me a paradigm of the *non sequitur* and an excellent caricature of many medical histories today, for the method I have just been describing is by no means as quaint and antiquated as I have made it sound. It is the current method in most general hospitals and in many private offices; although, in some, history taking is but a scanty business or is turned over to an office nurse who at the same time sizes up the patient's probable income.

Perhaps in a few places only has psychiatry made its inroads on the medical curriculum and modified this traditional way of taking histories. This is psychiatry's greatest contribution to clinical medicine, the introduction of what I have called elsewhere "scientific biography."

There is no doubt that a new type of medical history is being developed, though as yet it has not been formulated, and in only a few medical schools, to my knowledge, is it being deliberately taught. If such a change is occurring, it is, as I have said, largely due to the influence of modern dynamic psychiatry. But there are other reasons as well that have contributed to it.

The establishing of the germ theory of disease in the latter part of the last century set the pattern for much of the investigative work of the following half-century. Koch's laws became the Magna Carta of medical research. To isolate a germ and to prove its specific pathogenicity, this was the greatest scientific achievement. And why not? When one considers the triumphs and blessings that have resulted from such studies, it was natural that this type of thinking should have dominated clinical medicine and that in large measure it still does. The successes that were achieved have, as is well known, reduced the incidence of the infectious diseases and brought into relative prominence the degenerative diseases and the stress reactions. To these conditions such simple unitary etiological thinking, as exemplified by Koch's laws, seems far less applicable. We are no longer dealing with such invariable relationships as might be expressed in a simple syllogism. We have had to develop new theories and concepts of disease and also new methods of study.

Our aim in taking a medical history is no longer only to find an etiological agent and then to devise means of exorcising it. It is rather to discover what kind of individual we are dealing with, what are his strengths and weaknesses, his assets and liabilities, what his patterned reactions under stress, and in what respects do the bodily defenses which he mobilizes themselves turn into malign and damaging forces?

Harold Wolff has put this well when he says that, though man's protective activities may be lifesaving if they are used in emergencies to destroy the forces that threaten him, the same protective activities when used as lifelong patterns may damage the very structures which they were devised to protect.

Perhaps Shakespeare had a similar principle in mind when he had Hamlet say:

> Find out the cause of this effect,
> Or rather say, the cause of this defect,
> For this effect defective comes by cause.

Since in the modern world we are constantly being confronted by new and changing environmental situations and since the human organism has only a limited number of ways in which it can respond to these changes, it is clear that much of clinical medicine will be concerned with the problem of homeostasis. How does the organism strive to maintain a steady state, both psychologically and physiologically? Are its efforts effective and efficient? This is the general line of inquiry that a modern medical history must pursue. To do so, the form of the history has to be greatly revised. We have had pretty much to give up the question-and-answer game which some years ago led us so securely, at least so we thought, to our goals.

A wise physician today will recognize that in a great many instances he cannot possibly know just what questions to ask, and, furthermore, even if he did, the patient could not answer them. The taking of a medical history has become primarily a personal voyage of discovery into unknown territory. Physician and patient are joined in a common enterprise to uncover certain facts. Often the patient is a laggard and will resist progress, and as often the physician, because of his own emotional blindness, will not be able to see or understand what is before him.

This is true of a medical history as well as of a psychiatric one. In my opinion, there is not much difference between them except that imposed by time and by the emphasis of the immediate complaint. Since the medical history has become, or should become, at once more fluid and more elastic, no form or syllabus will really suffice, no printed list of queries against which one places check marks. These may have their value when one is engaged in a specific research project and is trying to get answers to certain set questions. Or, again, printed forms may have their uses in dealing with large numbers of patients when saving of time and medical personnel is of moment. But, important as such forms may be, I am not now concerned with them but rather with how this new method of history taking can be described, formulated, and taught.

Let us begin at the beginning. In spite of all our protestations about "the patient as a person," the young medical student still looks upon him as a case of this or that. If he does, it is our fault, because we still believe in a kind of Platonic abstraction called "disease," as if it existed independent of the body of the sufferer. The conventional and jejune introduction to most medical histories states that "the patient is a white male sitting comfortably in bed." The student seldom knows the patient's name, and, if he does, the national origin of the name means little to him. Actually, it makes a great deal of difference whether the patient is called Mr. Feitelbaum, Mr. Finnegan, or Mr.

Ford. As I look over some of my own records, I find such unconventional statements as Miss Smith looks like "a languid lily"; "Mr. Jones looks like a snapping turtle with a gold watch chain"; or, again, "Mr. T. is an artist of Finnish origin but with a Yankee accent. He looks like a pink-cheeked beer barrel." It is true that these are unscientific statements, that they introduce a subjective element which colors the material. But do not be deceived; it is quite impossible to keep out one's subjective judgments and opinions, and it is no gain in scientific accuracy to describe the patient as though he were a puppet.

It would be a great benefit to medical students if we could teach them the art of history taking in the medical outpatient departments. A bank teller and the corner grocer's wife cease to be themselves when we rob them of their usual plumage and put them into hospital nightclothes. Furthermore, they are different people when sitting opposite us in a chair from what they are when "lying comfortably" in a hospital bed. The very fact that a hospital bed is so strangely tidy and high from the ground makes them different from what they would be in their own bird's-eye maple or golden oak Grand Rapids variety.

What the student should see as clearly as he can is the patient's *persona,* i.e., what front does he present to the world? If he knows the patient's name and calls him by name, he will naturally get a more accurate picture of the patient because he will respond in a less guarded way. The student should then shake hands with him. This is not only a civil thing to do, but much can be learned from a handshake. Does the patient present the tips of his fingers only in an uncertain and limp way? Is he a bone crusher? Are the hands wet and cold and tremulous? Does the handgrasp cling lovingly as it does in many alcoholics? Or can the patient not release his grasp, as was true of one I saw the other day who was afflicted with a muscular dystrophy with pronounced weakness of extensor muscles?

Having established this contact, the student should be taught to exhibit some interest in the patient's welfare. It does not make much sense to approach a sufferer from a gastric ulcer and ask him right off the bat whether he was a breast baby or a bottle baby, even if this fact is important to ascertain. The patient should be encouraged to talk about the here and now, about what ails him. Why has he come to the hospital or come to consult the physician? Many present-day patients think that they are helping us most by giving a kind of prepared historical review of their lives, beginning with their parent's unhappy marriage and how they were jealous of their younger sisters. A colored cook recently said to me: "I have a terrible pain in the back, but I know it's all due to my inferiority complex."

The physician must go along with such comments but gradually lead his patient to talk about what ails him. It is far better to proceed from the present backward, although in the final write-up the history may be presented in reverse order. We must pay strict attention to how the patient behaves during the interview, to the language he uses, to his attitude toward his symptoms, to the anxiety with which they are associated. We must keep our ears cocked for what has been called "body language." What is the body trying to say that the patient cannot say?

During the course of such an examination we can include, without the patient's ever knowing it, certain of the usual psychological tests for memory, symbolization, logical faculty, and general intelligence. We do not need to have the patient say "Methodist Episcopal" in order to spot a dysarthria. We must above all get some knowledge of prevailing moods and suppressed emotions which may express themselves physiologically.

As I said at the beginning, what we are aiming at in taking a history is a knowledge of the person as well as of his illness because in most instances, perhaps in all, these are inextricably related. The method of what has been called "associative anamnesis" is a useful one. The patient is encouraged to talk freely. We interrupt him to guide him into productive channels, not by interposing new questions, but by picking up one of his own statements and modifying it just enough to rephrase it into a query that will serve as a new point of departure.

From the mass of material so obtained we try to reconstruct a life-history. We draw a map to help us find our way. But we must never forget that the map-making is a combined enterprise of patient and physician. It is for this reason, not for sentimental ones, that the physician-patient relationship is the basis both of history taking and of subsequent therapy.

CHAPTER VI

The Concerns of Psychiatry

PSYCHIATRY has made the headlines. It has even taken Hollywood by storm, or perhaps it would be more accurate to say that Hollywood has taken psychiatry by storm. As the war was largely responsible for the current burst of publicity, I will begin with a few comments on what we have learned from the war.

For two years, with a number of other psychiatrists, I worked in a rehabilitation clinic. The patients were almost all discharged servicemen. A few were young men who had been rejected by the Selective Service System because of severe psychoneuroses or other disorders of their personalities; a few of them were Wacs and Waves. When I started in, I expected to find cases of "shell shock," as we called them in World War I, or "battle fatigue," which is the name they were given in World War II. There were surprisingly few of them. By far the most frequent were restless, troubled, confused, irritable, and depressed individuals with a variety of physical symptoms, such as headache, indigestion, and palpitations. Many of them were in the midst of domestic difficulties with their parents or their wives. Others had a hard time settling down to work or finding a job at all to their liking. Still others were deeply disturbed by conflicts surrounding their sexual lives.

I soon got the impression that the clinic did not differ much from a civilian one or present problems unlike those which psychiatrists see in their private practices. There were, of course, exceptions. I recall one gaunt and hollow-eyed lad who had lain for ten days in a tent in the Philippines shaking with malarial chills. A tropical rain pelted down on him incessantly—punctuated only by Jap bombs. It was more than he could stand. He went into a kind of delirium—screamed and cried and had to be evacuated to the States. By the time I saw him, a month or so later, he had regained his composure and some of his lost weight. His malaria was under control with atabrine. He still jumped when someone slammed a door or when a car backfired. He was a little edgy and irritable, and he had horrible nightmares of bombings. He would awaken sweating and screaming with his heart pounding and with an enormous sense of relief to find himself safe in bed in his own home.

Although I have said that cases in a rehabilitation clinic and those in civilian practice are similar, this does not imply that there is no difference between military and nonmilitary psychiatry. Actually there is. Not only in the theater of operations, where "combat fatigue" is so common, but even in encampments at home, sudden, violent, disorganizing breakdowns occurred such as are seldom encountered among civilians unless they are severely psychotic. Sometimes these breakdowns cleared up surprisingly quickly after removal of the patient from the setting in which the illness began. Sometimes they required immediate active treatment—by methods which have not proved so successful in peacetime as in war.

One of these methods depends upon the use of certain narcotic drugs belonging to the group of barbiturates. These drugs have a sedative value by which they allay certain symptoms. They also make it possible for the therapist to gather important information, and they render the subject remarkably receptive to suggestion. By themselves, without active psychotherapy, both during their administration and after, they would accomplish little.

The two most frequently used are amytal and pentothal. Both are injected slowly into a vein in the arm until the patient becomes drowsy and his speech grows a little thick. In this condition he will often talk freely about what concerns him deeply, especially if he is prodded with an occasional question or if the doctor enters into the drama of the situation.

The opinion seems to be getting around, however, that all one needs to do is to give a person a shot of this "truth serum"—and all kinds of mental illness will be cured. That, of course, is far wide of the mark.

You will get some notion of what can be achieved in a "pentothal interview" from the following story:

A twenty-six-year-old infantry officer had been under severe mortar fire in the Kairuan Pass when a shell fell within a few yards of him. It killed his two noncommissioned officers and mutilated them horribly before his eyes. He was found wandering about the fields in a semistupor and remained so until he was hospitalized twenty-six days later. He was agitated, bewildered, frightened, and trembling all over. He could not give his name or recall what had happened to him.

At the slightest noise he started in terror, and his only word was "Who?"—uttered in a whispered voice. Under pentothal narcosis he recovered his forgotten experiences, recounting in detail the gruesome scene in which his companions were killed. This was no mere intellectual recapitulation. All the appropriate emotions swept over him. He lurched about the room searching for the two dead bodies. He cowered and trembled with fear and crouched on the floor as he might in his foxhole. Then he clenched his fists and threatened to kill "those bastards." At one point he buried his head in the medical officer's shoulder, suddenly smiled, and said: "I remember my name: it's Frank. I remember where I live. God, what a miracle that I can talk. I thought I'd never be able to, but I tried. I tried right along to talk and remember, but I couldn't. They must think I'm an awful baby. What will they do with me? I can't go back there." With the return of his speech came also rational behavior. He improved rapidly, though much anxiety and depression remained for a long time. He was finally sent home to his wife. It was felt that he would need further special treatment at home but that the ultimate outcome would be good.

This record, much condensed, was taken from that extraordinary document called *War Neuroses in North Africa: The Tunisian Campaign*, prepared by Lieutenant Colonel Roy R. Grinker, M.C., and Captain John P. Spiegel, M.C.

Despite the value of narcosis in the case cited, permanent cures are not achieved in any such dramatic way. What the drugs do accomplish is to remove those inhibitory influences which prevent disturbing emotions from expressing themselves except in indirect and oblique ways. If one jams a stopper into the spout of a kettle and sets it on to boil, it will have to blow its top. The inhibitory influences act as such a stopper, and the drugs help to remove it, so that steam can escape through normal channels. Blowing off steam does not in itself constitute cure, although it may be an important preliminary.

Not only was the young officer terrified by the explosion, but he felt intensely guilty that his two companions for whom he was responsible were slaughtered while he survived. As a soldier and an officer, he could not let his fear be seen, nor even acknowledge it to himself. The guilt over his own survival and the loss of his two friends were too distressing to bear.

The essence of the treatment in such cases depends on the sympathetic, understanding, and forgiving support of the doctor, who must know when to egg the patient on, when to call a halt.

Under certain conditions, hypnotism may be used in place of the barbiturates, as it was during the war in the

Pacific area and as it is, at times, in civilian practice. It has some advantages over the use of drugs and some disadvantages. Like them, it serves to free deeply buried and highly charged emotional material. Although it may cause the disappearance of symptoms, it seldom results in permanent cure. The same symptom may recur or another take its place. It is used, therefore, more to relieve certain distressing disorders of recent onset than as a method of effecting profound changes in personality.

Another means of combating extreme states of tension, anxiety, and panic is by the injection of small doses of insulin. In large doses it is used up to the point of loss of consciousness in treating schizophrenic patients. In another treatment for schizophrenia the drug metrazol was used to stimulate convulsions which have been found beneficial in certain mental illnesses. But convulsions are now brought about principally by electric shock, which has replaced metrazol and similar drugs. This form of convulsive treatment has come into wide use—probably far too wide. It should, of course, be administered by experts only. In certain selected cases it can achieve brilliant results. In others, especially if used excessively and in the wrong kinds of cases, it undoubtedly does harm. We are far from knowing all that we need to know about this subject, and there is still a good deal of disagreement among psychiatrists. There will continue to be until they understand how this method accomplishes its effects.

The therapeutic use of shock was stumbled on accidentally. It was found that certain patients suffering from depressions and from schizophrenic reactions, who also were afflicted with epilepsy, appeared to improve after a spontaneous convulsion. That led to the attempt to produce artificial convulsions by clamping two electrodes on the temples and sending a current of very low amperage through the brain. The whole thing lasts less than one minute, but the patient loses consciousness and has a convulsion exactly like an epileptic seizure. He may sleep for a short period thereafter. The confusion and loss of memory which follow gradually subside and there may be extraordinary improvement, especially in patients who are suffering from depressions.

These technics which I have outlined are not substitutes for the psychiatric interview, which remains the basis of most of our psychotherapy. An interview may be an orderly series of questions. More usually it is an apparently casual exchange in which the patient is encouraged to talk freely about what concerns him. In psychoanalysis, which I discuss in a later chapter, this method of undirected talk, or "free association," as it is called, is the guiding principle. It may lead into the world of dreams and revive forgotten memories of childhood. The physician must, of course, familiarize himself with the detailed history of his patient's life. He will talk with him about life at home, about relationships with wife and children, with parents and brothers and sisters, about jobs, friends, sexual behavior, eating and sleeping habits, bowel function, and about the experiences of childhood, and he will inquire, from the patient or his relatives, about the earliest habits of infancy.

Psychiatrists do ask the darnedest questions! But for good reason. Their aim is to discover and, above all, to help their patients understand, not just intellectually, but in a sense through their emotions, in what manner they react to stressful situations. What is the prevailing pattern of their behavior? Experiences damaging to some may not be to others. For one it may be the explosion of a land mine or a buzz bomb or the sinking of a ship by a torpedo; for another, exhaustion or physical illness—a threatened operation or an attack of grippe; for still another, the loss of a job or a new job with increased responsibility. Anything which shakes their security or jolts them out of their accustomed mode of adaptation may be sufficient to start a regressive process. They will then begin to exploit earlier, more childish methods of adaptation. These will in turn increase their difficulties and may lead eventually to a kind of withdrawal from the real world in favor of a fantasied one. Under such circumstances, no matter how excellent their intellects, no matter how high their I.Q.'s, they become increasingly crippled, increasingly incapable of plucking satisfaction out of the present. They cower helplessly in a hostile, threatening world; or they may strike out at the world in angry resentment.

Psychiatrists try to bring insight and understanding to such suffering people. Understanding does not come from lecturing and preaching. It may come if the relationship with the psychiatrist is a trusting and secure one, so that the patient dares expose himself to himself, so to speak. He may say: "I want to work this thing out for myself. I'm not crazy, I don't need to go to a psychiatrist. They're all nuts, anyway." These are familiar devices by which patients keep up their courage—and their symptoms. It is not for the psychiatrist to scout these devices. The most important thing he can do is to make himself available. His best ally is the patient's suffering and feeling of illness—better than the solicitude or insistence of friends and relatives.

In the Army, of course, it was different. Soldiers had no choice. If they were sent to a psychiatrist, they had to go. This had the advantage sometimes of insuring early treatment but the disadvantage of coercion. The psychiatrist was, after all, a medical officer with rank and with all the authority of the military hierarchy behind him—not in itself the basis of a good relationship. Nor did the Army ever free itself from the confused notion that psychoneurotics are malingerers—fakers. This notion is incorrect. But the reverse is true—malingerers (of which there were surprisingly few) are usually seriously disturbed people. Consistent with the Army's black-and-white, all-or-none principle, a soldier is either "crazy" or he is "not crazy." In the early part of the war the psychiatric wards were therefore "closed wards" where psychoneurotics, sufferers from stomach ulcer, and agitated, confused, perhaps delusional and hallucinating men were jumbled together.

If the Army made mistakes, it also made a great contribution to our understanding. We all owe an immense debt of gratitude to Brigadier General William C. Menninger and to his staff in the Surgeon-General's office. He had the opportunity of studying statistically facts which would be extremely difficult to come by in civilian life. That is one of the few good things that the ill wind of war has blown us. It has shown us, too, that the neuroses of war, the reactions to combat, are psychoneuroses based on previous emotional disorders, just as they are among civilians. This is an important fact. In war, as in peace, each one of us has his Achilles' heel—each carries a load of outer pressure and inner tension which, if added to, may cause a break.

This knowledge should make us more tolerant. It should encourage people to seek psychiatric help early—without delay. It should discourage self-administered treatment or, what is worse, meddlesome amateurish advice on the part of well-wishers. We should be ready to give up the vain hope of a miracle—in which the movies have so encouraged us. A change of air or a bottle of this or that or even a shot in the arm (or elsewhere) is probably not going to settle our emotional turmoil.

It is no service to psychiatry or to the public or to anyone not interested in box-office receipts to project on the screen a seductive female intern emotionally involved with a veteran who is "a victim of amnesia," as the papers have it. The veteran is finally cured by a nostalgic tune on the piano. Then the day breaks, the birds twitter, and he either does or does not marry the intern. Nor, again, is it useful or accurate to make the psychiatrist look like a Gestapo agent, putting his poor patient through a kind of third degree and, lacking only a short length of rubber hose, shocking a confession out of the sick man, who then miraculously recovers.

This kind of skeleton-in-the-closet psychiatry has dominated many of the attempts at popular dramatization. All we need to do, we are told, is open the door, let the sunlight pour in, and sweet reasonableness will come home to roost. Or, to change the figure of speech, if we thrust our probe or lancet into the abscessed mind, pus and corruption will discharge and mental health will follow. There is a misconception about this cleaning-out psychotherapy. It is based on the assumption, once believed to be true, that emotional catharsis—getting things off your chest—effects cures. Occasionally this is true; more often it is only a first step toward cure.

Final cure, as I have tried to emphasize, when achieved, results from a kind of "working-through" process in which the relationship with the psychiatrist is the touchstone. Successful treatment is a co-operative enterprise in which both partners, doctor and patient, play an active role. It is not like having a tooth out or an operation for appendicitis. Nor is the psychiatrist a demigod who works magic or a Svengali who practices a black and unsavory art on an innocent victim. Treatment can be compared to a journey of exploration through partly familiar, partly strange, country, in which the more experienced traveler acts as guide. If his companion refuses, or is unable, to open his eyes, he will come out none the wiser.

The psychiatrist must, therefore, be an honest man and a sound man and one to be trusted. And he must have had the necessary training and experience to deal with the intricacies and complexities of human relationships. He must, moreover, have time enough to take care of his patients and not charge them so much that they cannot afford to consult him. I shall have to admit right away that these specifications are far from realizable today. There are not nearly enough psychiatrists. Many of them are inadequately trained, and some are eccentric. But psychiatry has no monopoly on eccentrics, and eccentricity need not disqualify a man if he has arrived at some self-understanding.

The fact that we cannot now fulfil the needs that the war made all too clear is not our fault, nor is it reason to deny the needs. The more they are understood and appreciated and the greater the demand for adequate care of the emotionally disturbed, the more likely is it that these needs will be met.

Instead of a paltry three thousand or four thousand psychiatrists, we need nearer twenty thousand—and they must be trained not merely as custodians for the hopelessly insane but in all the technics of modern psychotherapy, especially in recognizing and learning how to treat psychoneurotic disorders. Important as the problem is, psychiatrists have always been chiefly concerned with the severe psychoses and have neglected the early detection and early treatment of less catastrophic illnesses. The opportunity is at hand for preventive psychiatry, but it can only come out of co-operation between the public and the profession. Funds must be made available, public as well as private. The curriculums of our medical schools must be modified so that young doctors, even those who do not intend specializing in psychiatry, will learn enough about these problems to recognize them and to treat the simpler ones themselves. Provision must be made for postgraduate education in psychiatry. A good deal is actually being accomplished in these directions, but more needs to be.

Psychiatrists are stepping down from their ivory towers. They welcome the exposure of the inhumanities practiced in some of our more backward state hospitals—horrible as they were. They welcome such organizations as the League for Epilepsy and the National Committee for Education on Alcoholism.

If you are still in doubt about the urgency of the problem of the mental and emotional health of the nation, let me give you some cold facts: Twelve out of every hundred candidates for Selective Service were rejected because of disorders of the personality. For each one hundred men rejected for all causes, thirty-nine were refused for this cause. In total figures, this represented one million six hundred thousand out of a lost manpower pool of four and a half million.

In terms of medical discharges from the Army, the neuropsychiatric patients constituted 41 per cent. There were three hundred and twenty thousand of them, and to this figure should be added another one hundred and thirty-seven thousand men separated from the service because of antisocial behavior, inadequacy, mental deficiency, and bed-wetting. There were over one million men admitted to the neuropsychiatric wards of our army hospitals, but of these only 7 per cent were actually "insane." Sixty to 70 per cent of the million were hospitalized because of psychoneurotic disorders, and for every one such man there were perhaps three treated outside of hospitals. Three out of five disability claims in the Veterans Administration are due to neuropsychiatric disorders, and the peak load of such patients will not be reached until 1975! This roughly was the situation in the Army, after screening and eliminating the unfit. And the Army is composed of the pick of the nation's crop.

In civilian life it is harder to furnish accurate statistics. Here, however, are some: Of all the hospital beds in America one-half are devoted to mental illnesses. In 1941 the total expenditures in state hospitals were $142,282,480. This figure represents the cost of the care of hospitalized psychotic patients only, of which there are some seven hundred thousand to a million. There are probably three to five million noninstitutionalized cases. This does not count the psychoneurotics in need of treatment and the run-of-the-mill medical and surgical patients in care of clinics and private doctors of whom some 50 per cent suffer from disturbances intimately connected with their emotional lives.

In the face of these overwhelming facts it is heartening to know that on July 3, 1946, President Truman signed the National Mental Health Act, originally introduced in the House of Representatives by Congressman J. Percy Priest of Nashville, Tennessee. The main provisions of the act are twofold: (1) to establish at a cost of $4,500,000 a National Psychiatric Institute for research into the prevention, cause, diagnosis, and treatment of psychiatric disorders and (2) to appropriate $10,000,000 per annum, or a sum sufficient to carry out this part of the act, for the purpose of making grants-in-aid to universities, hospitals, laboratories, and other public or private institutions and to individuals for research projects. Other important provisions of the act are to furnish financial assistance to states, counties, and localities to enable them to initiate adequate preventive mental health facilities and to train qualified personnel.

Administration of this program is vested in the Surgeon General of the United States Public Health Service and in a National Advisory Mental Health Council, consisting of six members appointed by him from outstanding authorities. These provisions have had the unqualified support of the leaders of psychiatric thought in the country. But it has been pointed out that mere expenditure of funds, however lavish, will not accomplish the ends of such a research institute; nor is any such institute better than its staff. What is required is brilliant leadership by the best brains attainable and a staff of men of first quality with training and character and a flair for original work. No collection of underpaid routineers will create more than a custodial home for patients on whom they may, to be sure, compile voluminous case histories. Ideas and new contributions in medicine do not spring from such sterile ground.

In such a large-scale program great caution must be taken not to sacrifice quality to quantity. There is no department of medicine which requires more skill and tact and greater personal integrity than the practice of psychiatry; nor can more damage be done by a bungler, even in surgery. To assure the training of suitably qualified men, the most careful and scrupulous selection should be practiced.

If the projected training program is to be successful and the level of psychiatric competence is to be raised throughout the country, then it will be essential to set up high standards both as to quality of personnel and as to the kind of training they are to receive. Adequate financial provision will have to be made for the trainees and their families.

The dearth of proper psychiatric clinics, both for adults and for children, even in our largest cities is lamentable. It is essential to increase their numbers and their staffs and to make them available for wage-earners during evening hours. Psychiatrists employed by such clinics must be adequately paid for their services. The practice of psychiatry moves at a slower pace than many other branches of medicine. It is clear that a psychiatrist who spends, let us say, forty-five minutes with a patient cannot see many patients in a working day. His colleague in medicine or surgery may treat three office patients to every one of his.

Present-day problems far transcend the scope and facilities of mental hospitals and psychiatric clinics. These problems have invaded the practice of medicine and the specialties and the work of our large general hospitals as well. It is here, and especially in pediatrics, that early difficulties are first encountered and that the ounce of prevention can best be administered.

I am not so naïve as to think that the millennium can be legislated in by act of Congress. The program we adopt must be a long-term one, pursued with patience and flexibility. The important thing is to start now and wisely. Some of my colleagues fear that psychiatry has been "oversold" to the public. I do not share this view. The truth cannot be oversold. Sensationalism, yes, and "nature faking." But not the truth. Here, too, it can set us free.

CHAPTER VII

Anxiety

THE war and the efforts to establish peace have brought to many of us a sharp realization of our anxieties. They are not new; they have always been with us. All kinds of men are subject to them—young and old, sophisticated and simple, civilized and savage, rich and poor, "neurotic" and "normal."

And yet if a psychiatrist asks a patient whether he suffers from feelings of anxiety, the chances are that the question will not be understood.

I will try to explain, to give some clearer idea of what this feeling is that grips men's hearts, corrodes their courage, robs them of decision, cheats them of rightful pleasures, causes them to become failures, gives rise to many bodily symptoms and disorders, makes them quarrel, lie, steal, kill, fall in love or out of love.

Anxiety is not the only force that propels us, but it is surely one of the most potent. It must be reckoned with if we want to understand ourselves or help others to understand themselves.

I have called anxiety a force. That is the first point I wish to make. It is not, of course, a physical force like steam pressure, the explosion of dynamite, or the pull of gravity. Anxiety is a psychological force, similar to that exerted by some emotions. We know, for example, that such emotions as rage and fear give rise not only to certain mental states but also to certain bodily reactions. These mental states would be hard to describe, though they are familiar to everyone. They are subjective experiences, more accessible to the language of poetry than of science. But the bodily reactions are felt and can often be detected by other people.

Charles Darwin in his book, *The Expression of the Emotions in Man and Animals*, has given an accurate and vivid picture of such reactions. In intense rage, for example, the face reddens and becomes purple, with the veins on the forehead and neck distended. The chest heaves and the dilated nostrils quiver. He speaks of "breathing out vengeance" and "fuming with anger." The body may be bent forward, with the limbs more or less rigid, the mouth closed with firmness, and the teeth clenched or ground together. In some instances the corners of the upper lip are drawn back and the teeth bared, which Darwin thought remarkable since men seldom use their teeth in fighting.

Most of us have at some time or other experienced great fright. The accompanying cold clammy hands, rapid breathing, pounding heart, feeling of goose pimples, and dry mouth are familiar sensations. Such reactions, although intense, are less chaotic and undesigned than they may appear to be. They are set in motion by well-understood chemical and physiological changes in the body, and they serve the purpose, as the late Dr. Walter B. Cannon has so brilliantly taught us, of preparing the organism for "fight or flight." The associated mental state, moreover, although explosive in intensity, is not wholly irrational. We are angry *at* someone because we have been hurt or slighted or insulted, or we are afraid *of* someone or something that has startled us. If we are making a trek through the jungle and suddenly hear the low growl of a tiger, it is quite rational for us to freeze in our tracks and to be stricken with terror. Or if we are walking on the sidewalks of New York and suspect that the man behind us is a thug with a blackjack, it is not unreasonable to take to our heels.

These intense emotional experiences have a way of discharging themselves, or they can be modified to some extent by self-control. In any case, after they have passed, they have passed. The mind and the body recover from their alerted states and regain their former equilibrium. There is no feeling of having lost one's mind, of having been afraid when there was nothing to be really afraid of. Now, the characteristic feature of anxiety is the reverse of this: we react with the bodily feelings of fear to situations that do not justify such reactions. If, for example, we visit a zoo and are overcome with terror by the sight of a tiger, safely caged and gazing at us with dreamy, indifferent eyes, then we are reacting with neurotic anxiety to a situation not in reality dangerous—but psychologically dangerous.

There are a great many such *phobic* reactions to which people are subject: fear, for example, of heights, of crowds, of subways, of trains, of snakes (of even a harmless garter snake), of going on the street alone, and so on. All these can be extremely uncomfortable and embarrassing, handicapping and distressing. They have one thing in common: they are irrational, that is, they are not to be explained by the actual situation.

This brings us back to our original inquiry. What is the irrational fear that we call "anxiety"? It is, first of all, a feeling of discomfort and distress. This distress is a signal to us that we are somehow in danger. But the danger, curiously enough, is not from without but from within. That is what gives to anxiety its strangely irrational and doubly distressing character. We are afraid of something going on within ourselves, of which we often have little or no knowledge. And, worse still, we cannot even begin to find out unassisted. It is like looking for a black cat in a dark room, where there is not one, as William James put it.

There are good reasons why the source of the danger within us should be inaccessible, why what Sir Osbert Sitwell calls "the warm palpitating twilight that lives beneath men's ribs or in the dreaming hollows, vast caverns, of their skulls" should be an unknown domain. We will come to those reasons presently. First, let it be noted that at the very appearance of the danger signal we jam on the brakes or we veer our course or we turn tail or we "explain" our discomfort and distress by some outward happening on to which we "project" our feeling or perhaps we become unaccountably irritable and angry or we may develop any one or more of a great variety of symptoms. All these reactions serve the purpose of relieving us of an intolerable tension by converting it into something else. The tension is in this manner diminished—drained off. Since the distress signal is thus met with an immediate automatic response which has as its purpose the lessening of distress, we may be aware of the response only and not at all of the underlying disturbance. All our attention is focused on the defenses against distress which may, to some extent, relieve us or substitute discomforts, more tolerable because more intelligible. But the symptom or the mood or the impulsive behavior is a red herring drawn across the trail which diverts us from discovering the true cause of our painful anxiety.

Most people have discovered for themselves ways of reducing nervous tension, so often an expression of concealed anxiety. One man will reach for his "favorite brand" and another for a drink. Some get relief from a warm bath or from hard physical exercise or from eating. These are perfectly legitimate ways of making life easier. But they do not always work. The relief may be too short-lived, and the method of achieving it may be habit-forming or otherwise harmful.

You have all seen the restless, tense chain smoker who cannot sit still or the man who has to have his drink and then another and another, until he begins drinking alone and insists on a nightcap. Before long he will need an eye opener too, and he is not really relaxed unless he is fuzzy in the head and half-seas over. Obviously this is no solution for his underlying anxiety, which remains with him when he is sober and is certainly not assuaged by his guilt and the mess he is making of his life.

Most fat people are fat because they eat too much. Constant hunger is often another expression of anxiety. Filling up on candy and other sweets may be, for some people, an attempt to get emotional satisfactions of which they feel deprived.

While anxiety frequently interferes with sleep, it causes some people, on the other hand, to need a great deal of sleep. They are comfortable only when they are unconscious. It makes work irksome and distasteful to some, but others are driven by an inordinate ambition or restlessness to exhausting labor. While one man becomes sexually impotent through anxiety, another needs constantly to reassure himself of his prowess by playing the Don Juan. So with women. One carries her virginal chastity to a cold grave, and another is loosely and experimentally promiscuous. It might surprise you to know that a very similar psychological mechanism may be at work in both types.

You will see that anxiety is a many-headed hydra, and you will understand now that when we ask a patient whether he suffers from feelings of anxiety, he will hardly know what we are talking about—shortness of breath, yes, or palpitations or nausea and vomiting or intestinal upsets or headaches and dizziness or sleeplessness and horrible nightmares or alcoholic sprees, or temper tantrums or fear of losing his mind or even alien, plaguing obsessional thoughts. These he acknowledges and knows all too well. But they are derivative—the unwanted children of unknown parents.

It is not always so. Some patients come to us complaining that they have uncomfortable feelings of unexplained and senseless fear. They will say: "It's foolish. I have nothing to be afraid of. I have everything to be grateful for—a good husband and fine children and a happy home life, not even any money worries. Still I'm always scared to death."

Others will fairly burst into our offices as if the devil were after them, their eyes popping, their foreheads drenched with sweat, trembling all over, and nearly speechless. They are entirely unaware of what is pursuing them. So, often, are we. But we can draw inferences from their behavior and their chance remarks. With such patients we proceed with caution. If we try to unfold to them even the lightest word of their tale, we may plunge them into a panic, and they will run away from us as precipitately as they ran to us for help. Or they may be forced to seek escape from their terror by killing themselves or even someone else. Such people need to be protected. They may need to be hospitalized and treated with sedative or narcotic drugs or with "subcoma" doses of insulin. Only after the storm abates can we begin to approach the source of their difficulty.

Some people lend themselves to such an exploration; others do not. Instead, they mobilize new and stubborn defenses against a realization of their anxiety. Depending upon the character of the patient, the strength of his personality, the severity of his symptoms, we use varying therapeutic technics. These may be of a supportive nature, in which we aim to fortify the personality and, by reassurance, to allay the symptoms. Or we may use uncovering technics in which we relentlessly track the monster to his lair. We then aim to expose the underlying anxiety, but in small doses, so that the sufferer can tolerate it and build up a kind of active immunity against it. Such an enterprise may be difficult and protracted. Sometimes, nevertheless, there is a blessed relief from nervous tension, a new orientation toward the real world, a greater capacity to work, to love, and to pluck durable satisfactions from the day.

What, then, is this thing that bedevils us? It is a ghost, an anachronistic ghost. Like Hamlet's father's ghost, "doomed for a certain term to walk the night, till the foul crimes done in my days of nature are burnt and purged away." What are these crimes, and when did we commit them?

There can be little doubt that the seeds of anxiety are sown in early childhood, when our own helplessness, our bodily needs, and our utter dependence on grownups for their fulfilment awaken in us reactions of longing, despair, resentment, and rage—too intense for us to manage.

We owe much of our understanding of this still obscure subject to the psychoanalytic studies of Freud. In 1926 he set down his considered formulations. Among them we find such statements as this:

> Only a few instances of the expression of anxiety in infancy are intelligible to us. . . . Thus, the three situations of being left alone, being in the dark, and finding a strange person in place of the one in whom the child has confidence (the mother), are all reducible to a single situation, that of feeling the loss of the loved (longed for) person.

Anxiety is then conceived of as an expression of helplessness: "as if," says Freud, "the still very undeveloped creature did not know what else to do with his longing."

Perhaps this is the armature on which our subsequent

anxieties are wound—this primal fear of abandonment, this craving for protective care. When you consider that an infant's survival depends wholly upon the care of others, it is easy to understand why its bodily needs for food and warmth find such insistent and imperious expression and why a comforting, all-providing mother becomes the chief object of its longing. Her presence means life, her absence death.

It was Freud's daughter, Anna Freud, who showed in the cataclysmic experiment of the London blitz that separation from its mother was the greatest trauma to the young child, greater than the perils of the blast or the subsequent homelessness and privation. Often the small child enjoyed the wholesale destruction unless his mother gave signs of terror—an emotion quickly conveyed to him. Of course, if the mother is a cold, ungiving, stern, and disciplinary one, she may be a bane and not a balm, and she may augment these basic infantile anxieties.

Mounting physical tensions, unsatisfied cravings, are a quick warning, a precursor to the cry for help. They themselves are felt as anxiety. And this pattern remains with us throughout life, buried in an unconscious part of ourselves. Here, then, is the irrational ghost that walks and squeaks and gibbers when occasion beckons.

This primal, basic anxiety is present in all of us. Whether it is laid to rest or easily aroused will depend upon many factors—hereditary, constitutional, and experiential—and may determine to what extent we are prone to psychoneurotic illness.

Though no one can longer deny the enormous importance of the first few months and years of life in setting the stage for later neurotic disturbance, it would be a mistake to lose sight of the significance of the immediate life-situation. In dealing with so complicated a subject as human emotions there is always a temptation to oversimplify, to reduce it to a schematic system. This may make it comfortable for us because we have the feeling of having arrived at an "explanation," but, on the other hand, it may represent a distortion of fact.

Anxiety as we see it in our patients is usually the outcome of some actual conflict in their lives. The conflict most frequently lies between a strong emotional instinctive urge and an equally strong prohibition of conscience. The resultant friction of these opposed forces is felt as tension or anxiety. I could cite innumerable examples of this:

A young woman, whose husband is wholly preoccupied with his profession and never makes love to her, is seized with jitters and with feelings of faintness at the most inopportune times. She is a gentle and sweet woman, but her deep resentment has been aroused, which she needs to keep in check. She is hardly aware of it, but she has reacted to the conflict with these unpleasant feelings.

A middle-aged man cannot go on the street except in the company of his wife and a young male companion. If he were forced to do so, he would break out into a real panic. Unknown to himself he has strong unconscious homosexual leanings against which he has to protect himself. As long as he is chaperoned—and it is noteworthy that he needs a chaperon of each sex—he is moderately comfortable, but not so when he is alone on the street. Then the possibility of giving in to his hidden wishes is too imminent.

A young girl had been kissed by a lad and sexually aroused by him. She reacted to this experience with the conviction that she was pregnant and with attacks of uncontrollable nausea and vomiting. Her own sexual needs and impulses have run head on into her strict conventional upbringing. The conflict which followed is expressed in her symptoms, and they in turn conceal from her the real problem.

Or, again, there is the man whose strict father, with whom he was at constant swords' points, suddenly died of a heart attack in his presence. Following this misfortune the son lost interest in his job, became sleepless, morose, and withdrawn, and had no energy or zest. The hostile feelings toward his father, mobilized through his sudden death, were immediately suppressed because of bad conscience. Again we see the resulting onset of symptoms.

A last instance of anxiety resulting from a conflict of forces is the case of the able, ambitious young business executive—the white-haired boy of his organization. He is, in fact, an insecure, dependent sort of person but admirably "compensated" on the surface. He was promoted to a new and responsible position with a boost in salary—everything he wanted. He should have been in clover. Instead he went to pieces. He developed dizzy spells and palpitations. He worried over trivial things, and he was most unhappy when his wife was not there to comfort and reassure him. In this situation the chief conflict lay between strong dependent needs and a compensatory effort toward independence and success.

As I have said before, the war showed anew that each one of us has his Achilles' heel, each his breaking point, each his stress tolerance. For some the limit is quickly reached. A soldier's camp, away from home and his accustomed civilian surroundings, may be enough to lower the barrier and flood the man with an unmanageable panic; or, more usually, it may bring on frequent minor illnesses—often mistaken for malingering. But for others the explosion of a land mine, the loss of buddies, the incessant mud and fatigue and pounding of artillery fire, or frequent exhausting and perilous missions through flak may be the determining and inciting cause of neurotic illness. Even in such cases, however, we must look beyond for the underlying anxiety. The most frequent source of conflict lies between instinctive fear of battle and the inner command to be brave.

Each one will break according to his kind. Men are like crystals. When they are struck a blow, they fall apart in certain planes, depending upon their inner structure and the tensions by which they are held together. For some a gentle tap is enough. Others can withstand the blow of a sledgehammer.

At each point in man's slow and uncertain development from infancy to adulthood this pervading anxiety may emerge for a while or be forced back again or lead to a symptom. Or it may pop up in the disguise of some aberrant behavior such as delinquency and crime. Like a subterranean stream it constantly appears above the surface and disappears again. Anxiety may attach itself to any bodily function. It may invade, and often does, the sexual life, where it produces disabilities and perversions. It may come between man and his conscience and between man and his fellows. It may disrupt marriages or precipitate ill-considered ones. Because man is engaged in a constant battle against anxiety, shadowboxing with an enemy that he cannot see, he often strikes out at the world, to no purpose, in a resentful, cantankerous, and aggressive way.

If his load of anxiety is not too great, if he is able to keep it at bay, so that it does not intrude itself too much into his person and disturb his physical, intellectual, or emotional functioning, then he may escape neurotic illness and be one of those normal people who pride themselves on being normal. They have been called "normopaths"—perhaps facetiously, but with some discernment. Like all human beings they, too, carry on a struggle, although a victorious one. If they can love and work and play to their own satisfaction *and that of others*, then they are normal enough for all practical purposes. We psychiatrists get the impression that they are a small company, a "happy few." It is our greatest task and concern that they increase in numbers.

Whether psychiatry alone will ever solve the problem of anxiety is doubtful. It appears to be inherent in our culture, if not in our nature. A far greater understanding is necessary than we now possess. Perhaps that will come from the co-operative efforts of anthropologists, educators, psychologists, psychiatrists, and sociologists. But important, too, in reaching such understanding is a general awareness of how vital this subject is to our hopes and plans for peace and the good life.

CHAPTER VIII

Psychoanalysis

SINCE the beginning of this century psychiatry, like clinical medicine, has concerned itself more with the causes of disease than with its description and classification. In other words, it has become more dynamic in its approach. As medicine had its great masters of description, like Sydenham, so psychiatry had its Kraepelin.

The birth of modern psychotherapy can be traced to France with the work of Liébault, of Bernheim, and of Charcot. The effect of their observations is by no means yet spent. It has profoundly influenced all of modern psychiatry. It was to Charcot's clinic at the Salpêtrière that Freud came as a student-physician in 1885. Here it was that he witnessed the experiments with hypnotism on hysterical patients. Although Freud always acknowledged Charcot as his "venerated teacher," he paid tribute as well to Liébault and to Bernheim of the Nancy school for their "extremely impressive demonstrations" of suggestion.

Almost one hundred years earlier an Austrian physician, who had studied in Vienna, having made experiments on the supposed curative power of the magnet, brought his theory of animal magnetism with him to Paris where he devoted himself to curing disease. This was Franz Anton Mesmer, for whom the occult art of mesmerism was named. His séances were investigated by a commission of physicians and scientists appointed by the French government. They denounced him as an impostor. Only one of them dissented. This was the botanist, A. L. de Jussieu, who wrote a minority report. He was convinced that an investigation into the forces behind animal magnetism would be highly illuminating, and he realized that imagination was an important factor in Mesmer's séances.

One of the commission was Benjamin Franklin, who agreed with the majority in their conclusion that "some sick persons of the common people are the only ones who feel any effects of animal magnetism." Lacking his usual shrewd perspicacity, he fell in with his colleagues' exclusive demand for physical proofs, and he missed thereby the opportunity of becoming the discoverer of modern psychology. But Franklin then was old, in poor health, and completely absorbed by his diplomatic duties. Mesmer himself did not understand what lay behind animal magnetism, not even when D'Elson, his French protagonist, in a response to the Academy's report, declared: "The new agent might indeed be no other than imagination itself, whose power is as extensive as it is little known. . . . If treatment by the use of the imagination is the best treatment, why do we not make use of it?" It has been said that "with these words Dr. Charles d'Elson laid the cornerstone of modern psychotherapy."

The learning that, in its crude form, had been brought from Vienna to Paris by Mesmer was returned, considerably refined, nearly a century later by Freud, who took it from Paris back to Vienna. There he urged the internist Josef Breuer to resume the "cathartic procedure," which had remained dormant for a number of years, and there, too, Freud, having been disappointed with the successes of electrotherapy, turned to treatment by suggestion in deep hypnosis. As is well known, Freud for a while joined forces with Breuer. The fundamental fact of Breuer's discovery was, to use Freud's own words, that "the symptoms of hysterical patients depend upon impressive, but forgotten scenes of their lives (traumata). The therapy founded thereon was to cause the patients to recall and reproduce these experiences under hypnosis (catharsis), and the fragmentary theory deduced from it was that these symptoms corresponded to an abnormal use of undischarged sums of excitement (conversion)." This theoretical conception was the joint product of Breuer's and Freud's minds. It represents the cornerstone on which the subsequent structure of psychoanalysis was erected.

Psychoanalytical theory was derived empirically and inductively from observation. It has, therefore, the structure of a science and can be taught. It is not a philosophy of life, and Freud resisted all efforts to elevate or derogate it into a "system." He once said: "I learned to restrain speculative tendencies and, following the unforgotten advice of my master, Charcot, I looked at the same things again and again until they, themselves, began to talk to me." For this reason, although undoubtedly for personal ones too, Freud fought those among his pupils, like Adler, Jung, and Rank, who seceded from him and who struck out on their own to formulate other theories. While some of these attempted to analyze the unconscious, I shall here discuss only the pioneer Freudian method to which alone the term "psychoanalysis" is legitimately applied.

What Freud did was to discover a new method of investigating the psychic life. The method known as "free association" was the natural outgrowth of the cathartic procedure which Freud gradually abandoned because he found the original traumatic theory an inadequate explanation of psychoneurosis, and therapy by hypnotic abreaction of little permanent value. The "cure" under hypnosis was, moreover, purely a symptomatic one and depended on maintaining a personal relationship between patient and physician. What Freud discovered is now pretty generally known, namely, that patients will reveal, even when awake, many important things concerning themselves, if the physician listens attentively and sympathetically. But Freud listened as attentively to the apparent irrelevancies as he did to more reasoned utterances, especially when they were accompanied by evidences of emotion. In applying this passive attention to his patients' outpourings, Freud soon observed that thoughts are not always connected in the logical and orderly sequence of usual conversation. If the patient is sufficiently relaxed and confident, his thoughts will tumble out in a manner that at first does not seem to make sense. It is to Freud's credit that he discovered the rhyme and reason behind these apparently unrelated thoughts. He concluded that logical conscious thinking depended upon the constant exclusion of intruding thoughts. These are kept out of focus or "repressed" because they seem illogical, trivial, embarrassing, repugnant, or because they may undermine self-esteem. Freud, therefore, demanded of his patients that they try to lay aside for the moment all self-criticism and that they make the effort to be as truthful as possible by relating *everything* that came into their minds. He discovered that their flow of ideas had, indeed, a kind of inner logic, that ideas which seemed to pop up at random were connected by the feelings, attitudes, and emotions of the thinker.

This discovery led to the necessity of constructing the theory of an unconscious mental life, often quite remote and unrelated to the conscious life of everyday. He conceived of the unconscious as a "special region of the mind" —not, of course, anatomically located—where thoughts, feelings, impulses, wishes, and instinctual drives existed, blind and inarticulate. Here they exerted a kind of pressure for expression in order to relieve the tension which they set up. This pressure for expression revealed itself in the seemingly chance verbal productions of his patients and also in their behavior, gestures, memory defects, slips of the tongue, their occupations and preoccupations, and often in the symptoms of which they complained. It was with this method of free association that Freud set out to explore the unconscious mind.

If one may be permitted to use the expression "unconscious thinking," it can be said that thinking at this level is of a much more primitive, infantile order than is usual conscious thinking. For example, the laws of nature do not prevail; time and space relationships have no validity; gravity does not exert its accepted pull (how often in dreams do people fly over housetops!); one and the same person can be both loved and hated or can be substituted for another, because of some slight physical resemblance or because of a similarity in feeling toward them; one part of the body is often displaced by another; long-abandoned beliefs in magic and fairy stories are freely resorted to, and many feelings and emotions never achieve ideational content at all but express themselves by bodily sensations or by the discharge of the vegetative nervous system. So, hate may express itself in the form of diarrhea, stubbornness by constipation, disgust by vomiting, and fear by a great variety of bodily disturbances, without any of the underlying emotions or affects, as they are called in psychiatry, ever making themselves more directly apparent.

The task of the psychoanalyst, then, is to learn the language of the unconscious so that the hidden forces (libido) in his patient become known to him and can be liberated for productive living rather than for the formation of symptoms. Freud speaks of pursuing the libido "in the analytic treatment, aiming always at unearthing it, making it accessible to consciousness and at last serviceable to reality." To learn this language requires, like the language of any science, a long period of study. The best and the essential preparation is for the student himself to have been analyzed. This will give him a familiarity and an "at homeness" with his own unconscious processes and will enable him, by just so much, to understand his patients.

The most direct approach to the unconscious will be found in dreams, where this primitive type of thinking, already alluded to, is so outspoken. Freud soon learned to distinguish between the manifest content of a dream, usually expressed in the idiom of the dreamer's daily life, and its latent or hidden content, which can be deciphered only through obtaining the ideas associated with the imagery of the dream.

For example: A patient dreamed of a small alligator, which vomited blood all over the keyboard of a piano. This, the manifest content, meant nothing to the patient, but she recalled that at the age of twelve she had had a pet alligator, which she used to dress up in doll's clothes and wheel about in a doll carriage. She could do nothing more with the thought of vomiting blood, until the analyst, piecing together the age of twelve and the probable onset of menses, suggested that the vomiting of blood on the piano keys (a good example of displacement of one organ by another) perhaps referred to some menstrual accident. The patient then recalled the sudden hemorrhage which a governess had experienced while in her company, and only the next day did she remember that once, when she was at the circus with her mother and her three younger brothers, her mother had left a pool of blood in the chair of the box which they occupied. The little girl did not know just what this meant, but she was frightened by it and took great pains to conceal the occurrence from her brothers. This patient's mother is an accomplished pianist, who was introduced into the dream by the image of the keyboard.

This abridged version of a dream, only partially analyzed, and its manifest and latent content give some notion of the extraordinarily condensed and distorted character of the language of the unconscious. Sometimes it can be understood only by inference and reconstruction, just as an archeologist reconstructs a pot from a small shard or a skull from a mandible or as a geologist reads the past from present erosions or from the impression that fossils have left in rocks. There will often be something of the happy guess in dream interpretation, but the wise and experienced analyst never foists his interpretation on a patient. He throws out a well-timed suggestion based on the evidence at hand with the hope that further associations will be evoked and that a piece of forgotten biographical material will come to light. When this occurs, the patient usually feels that something has "clicked," or, on the other hand, if sensitive material is being approached, he may have need to reject the interpretation completely. The art of analysis depends greatly on the proper timing of interpretations. In any case, the purpose of interpretation is not primarily to unearth a traumatic experience, as Breuer set out to do in his cathartic method. It is rather to remove resistances so that the patient will continue to associate freely and thus gradually revive the prevailing affective attitudes of his infancy and childhood. Although "resistance" is the chief stumbling block to analysis, from another point of view it is the essential material with which we work. It is the mountain through which we dig our tunnel or the rock through which we drill our well.

Anyone who uses the free-association method will quickly become aware of the fact of resistance. In spite of the most conscientious efforts, on the part of the patient, to tell everything, he cannot be completely successful in this enterprise. Certain thoughts are almost automatically "repressed" or sucked back into unconsciousness. Patients find themselves unable to talk, or they will babble along about the trivialities of their daily lives. There are innumerable ways in which resistance betrays itself to the analyst. They may run the gamut from forgetting appointments or being late to concerted efforts on the part of the patient to ingratiate himself with the analyst or to impress him or to lead him into theoretical and philosophical discussions. Anything to draw a red herring across the trail. All the while the patient, although ostensibly and honestly trying to co-operate, is fighting to keep from his mind the very things he is also striving to reveal. These are not usually the peccadilloes and indiscretions or even the vices of adult life. They are much more likely to be what was originally on the surface in childhood but kept secret to avoid adult reproof, thoughts and feelings, fantasies and emotions, often intimately bound up with such simple bodily activities as sucking, biting, defecating, and urinating. It is through these functions that the infant establishes his first contacts with the world of objects around him, functions which are used not only to satisfy bodily needs but to express emotions. And foremost in emotional importance in this world, because his survival depends upon her, looms the figure of his mother, who may become to the patient in later life the unconscious prototype of all other women. Father and brothers and sisters and nurses play their vital role too and remain forever the characters which people the drama of his maturity. With its genius at legerdemain the unconscious can play tricks and substitute teachers and employers for fathers, colleagues and rivals for siblings, wives and sweethearts for sisters and mothers. Even the sex of the individual does not hinder his being displaced or substituted by another. The unconscious thinks nothing of introducing a man for a woman or vice versa, if there is some slight similarity between them or if the feeling toward them is analogous.

Bearing this in mind, the analyst will not be surprised to find that he himself soon takes on in the patient's thoughts, attributes and characteristics which he may not in reality possess. The patient makes of him what he needs him to be. This is all the truer because proper analytical technic depends on the physician's keeping his own personality, his predilections and moral judgments, out of the relationship. The patient then projects his feelings and needs onto the analyst and tries to make him conform to his own fantasy. This phenomenon, so surprising to the tyro and to the patient alike, is known as "transference," so called because the patient transfers to the analyst feelings and attitudes actually belonging elsewhere, usually to important persons connected with his childhood. In this unusual relationship the patient loses, in greater or lesser degree, the common-sense, realistic attitude of an intelligent human being seeking cure of an illness and instead shifts to a neurotic one in which childish and emotional features may predominate. From these neurotic attitudes the analyst tries to extricate his patient. Such attitudes need not immediately make their appearance. The patient may begin with eagerness to conquer his difficulties; he may be acutely aware of his neurotic handicaps and be ready to go to great lengths by sacrificing both time and money to overcome them; and yet, gradually and subtly, this attitude gives way to another one. He appears now to be indifferent to the outcome of the treatment. He may become touchy, irritable, flirtatious, demanding, and spend his time battling with the analyst and trying to trick him into doing what he does not intend to do. His reason for coming to analysis is no longer to get well but rather to extract some kind of emotional satisfaction from the treatment. He wants to be waited on, taken care of, advised as to major or even minor decisions, helped in practical matters, and generally reassured, praised, comforted, and loved.

In one form or another this period, known as the "transference neurosis," occurs in every analysis of normal as well as neurotic people. It is a time when the emotions which they are experiencing are more important to them than is recovery. During this period they appear to be dominated by the major, unresolved, unconscious problems of their childhood. These are reproduced and lived out in the transference situation, the patients striving always to get what they failed to get in childhood or never learned to do without. Recovery depends upon working through this complicated relationship that contains within it the original infantile conflict.

In a sense the "transference neurosis" is an artifact, experimentally produced in the analytical situation; or, rather, it is a condensed, telescoped version of the patient's life-history in which his prevailing conflicts, discontents, and the imperious unrealistic demands of his childhood are revived and exposed. This gives the analyst the opportunity to deal with them, in pure culture, so to speak, and in a more or less controlled situation, because many of the difficulties which neurotic individuals experience in life have to do with their relations to others, and these are now centered largely on the person of the analyst.

It is a period, therefore, in which the patient often becomes sicker. His symptoms may increase, and he may develop new ones. This is painful for him, but he relinquishes his fantasies with great reluctance. He even enlists his most intense love feelings toward the analyst, not to co-operate with him, but, as further resistance, demanding, sometimes even expecting, immediate gratification rather than ultimate cure. The proper and skilful handling of this situation requires tact, subtlety, and a clear-sighted steadiness of purpose on the part of the analyst. He strives always to see behind the intensity of his patient's feelings, recognizing in his inordinate need to be loved, evidences of anxiety or other overwhelming emotion such as hate or guilt. His calm and steadying presence finally makes it possible for the patient to come to grips even with these devastating feelings.

The term "transference neurosis," as here used to designate a certain phase of analytical treatment, was used also by Freud in a kind of diagnostic sense. Those people capable of reacting in the manner described were said to be suffering from a "transference neurosis," a category including the chief psychoneurotic illnesses, especially those of the hysterical, phobic, and obsessive-compulsive types. These Freud distinguished from the "narcissistic neuroses," schizophrenia, for example, which Freud believed did not lend themselves to this kind of therapy because they were incapable of developing a transference neurosis. We now know that many other individuals besides those suffering from hysteria or obsessive-compulsive neuroses are capable of developing and experiencing intense transference relationships. This holds true for some schizophrenics, for example, who are not too lost in their autistic fantasies. It is also true of certain manic-depressives, when they are neither too elated nor too depressed. And it is also known that so-called "neurotic" characters, psychopathic personalities, epileptics, and a variety of other mentally or emotionally disturbed people react with intense transference feelings, from which, however, it may be far more difficult to extricate them than it is in the psychoneurotic group. It was for this group that the method of psychoanalysis was originally designed.

There is reason to believe that transference is a far more widely distributed phenomenon than is to be gleaned from technical treatises alone. Even normal love partakes of it. Much of the exaggerated ecstasy of falling in love contains within it some of this tendency to project onto the loved one attributes which we need him to possess. The blindness of love consists not in loss of vision but in a kind of selective vision. We see what we want and need to see. And the raiment in which we clothe the one we love is made up of the visions of our childhood. The good wife then becomes mother, sister, nurse, companion, courtesan, all rolled into one; and the good husband, father, brother, friend, even mother. But in much less intense emotions than those of love this same process can be seen at work. In the relationship of teacher and pupil, of lawyer and client, of priest and parishioner, of officer and men, of political leader and constituents, of orator and audience, of dog and master—in all of them the authority and magic and power of the one is derived in part from the projected needs of the other. If this is true in these situations, how significantly true is it of the physician and the surgeon whose power to heal depends in such large measure on the personal relationships which he establishes with his patients. Much of the success of his therapy will depend on these imponderables.

If, then, the tendency to form transference is ubiquitous in man, it alone cannot be used as a criterion for the application of psychoanalytic therapy. The method has been applied extensively both here and abroad to almost the whole category of mental and emotional illness. Analysts vary greatly in their willingness to apply it to others than the classical psychoneurotic group for which it was intended. The rash and the courageous, the resourceful and the imaginative, will often take on cases that the conservative and the cautious will shun. This is probably also true of surgeons, although in their work prognosis is more soundly based on statistical data than in the case of psychoanalysis.

It is, of course, desirable to have arrived at a tentative diagnosis and to have some notion as to what outcome may be expected before beginning psychoanalytical treatment. These facts are learned from an ordinary psychiatric interview. Some analysts have found that a too exhaustive preliminary investigation interferes with the patient's subsequent willingness or ability to talk freely. Many modern analysts enlist the help of clinical psychologists whose methods of testing sometimes afford remarkable insight into the nature of the difficulty. When the decision has been made to use the psychoanalytical method, the patient is briefed in detail as to what is expected of him. The number of visits per week are agreed upon. They may be as many as five or six. Fewer than three are usually not practicable, because so much material accumulates that the analyst will have difficulty in not losing the thread. The matter of fees is frankly discussed. Analysts' fees are, as in the case of other physicians, usually adjusted to the patient's income. But, since each visit lasts from fifty to sixty minutes, the number of patients an analyst can see in a day is, of course, much more limited than is the case with many other medical specialists. Accordingly, most analysts find it difficult to accept more than a very few patients at low fees. This is unfortunate but unavoidable. Endowed clinics where psychoanalysis can be carried out with patients of the lower income brackets are urgently needed. Once the hour and fee have been agreed upon, it is expected that both patient and physician will abide by this agreement. Some analysts charge their patients even when they do not come. This has its good reasons, but it is by no means an invariable rule.

In order that the patient may be put at ease, he is usually asked to recline on a couch. This has the double advantage of allowing the patient to relax and sparing him the embarrassment of constantly looking at the physician and being looked at by him. A reclining position on a couch is not necessary to analysis, but it is a great help when the method of free association is employed.

From the start the patient is urged to talk freely about the things uppermost in his mind. He is, at the same time, constantly encouraged to allow his mind to return to the events and feelings of his childhood. When dreams begin to be recounted, they are dealt with in relation to the patient's present life-situation, but they are also used to expose and reveal buried memories. Technical language is not used by the experienced analyst, who usually cautions his patient, at least in the earlier phases of the treatment, not to read psychoanalytical treatises. Nor does he enter into theoretical discussions with him. He usually recognizes these discussions as a form of resistance.

The patient and his relatives are naturally greatly concerned as to how long the treatments will last. This is a prediction not easy to make. It depends upon a number of variable factors; not least important are the patient's willingness and capacity to change and the analyst's sensitiveness and skill. The treatment seldom lasts less than a year; sometimes, in stubborn and difficult cases, much longer. Cure is not achieved necessarily as soon as the patient appears to have recovered. But the final proof of the pudding will be the eating. As Kubie put it, "It is fair to measure its results in terms of the patient's happiness and peace, his pleasure in activity, his freedom from disturbing states of depression, anxiety, guilt, fear, or jealousy, and more particularly his freedom from the special neurotic symptoms which may have brought him to analysis."

Our criteria for recommending analysis in preference to other forms of psychotherapy are still not sufficiently sharp. Certain factors must always be taken into account. They are well summarized by Hendrick in his valuable book, *Psychoanalysis: Facts and Theories*. He lists among them age and general intelligence, strength of character, and also what is called "secondary gain." This latter refers to "those pleasures which a psychoneurotic person seeks to derive from or win by his symptoms or character traits." He states, quite correctly, that these pleasures are not the cause but rather the result of the illness. Hendrick finally emphasizes the importance of considering the real situation in which the patient finds himself. If this is too threatening or destructive to the patient and if he is caught by fate in a situation from which he cannot extricate himself, our efforts to help him by analysis probably will be thwarted. One would not attempt to analyze a starving, brutalized inmate of a prison camp, no matter how neurotic he was.

Although such qualities as intelligence and strength of character may be judged on practical, empirical grounds, we now are in possession of certain methods which can give us a more quantitative appraisal of them. Intelligence tests and projective technics such as the Rorschach and the thematic apperception tests of the clinical psychologists are proving of value in the selection of those patients suitable for analysis. Sometimes, however, we need to resort to a trial period of a month or six weeks, a kind of shakedown cruise, in which we explore the personality. During such a period the negative factors in prognosis will often become manifest.

From what has been said it must be obvious why it is so difficult to estimate the results of analysis or to build up a body of significant and reliable statistics. We are dealing with a subject in which the variables are incalculable, not least among them being the skill, native ability, and resourcefulness of the analyst himself, even assuming him to have fulfilled all the stringent and necessary requirements of his training. Still, for those demanding statistical evidence, whatever its value, data can be found in the reports of the Berliner Psychoanalytisches Institut, of the London Clinic of Psychoanalysis, and of the Institute for Psychoanalysis, Chicago. The results obtained in private practice have never been adequately evaluated and summarized.

There are many points still at issue among analysts. In Freud's own words:

> Psychoanalysis has never claimed to give a perfect theory of the human psychic life, but has only demanded that its discoveries should be used for the completion and correction of knowledge we have gained elsewhere. . . . It may, therefore, be said that the psychoanalytic theory endeavors to explain two experiences, which result in a striking and unexpected manner during the attempt to trace back the morbid symptoms of a neurotic to their source in his life-history; viz., the facts of transference and of resistance. Every investigation which recognizes these two facts and makes them the starting-points of its work may call itself psychoanalysis, even if it leads to other results than my own.

The definition of what psychoanalysis is and what it is not should now be clear, and there is no justification for using the term loosely or applying it where it does not belong. The door is left open for further experimentation, for efforts to shorten this often tedious and costly process, for extending its field into psychotic and psychosomatic illness, for combining it with hypnosis and the use of drugs. It is the method itself which has value and which was Freud's great contribution, because it has given us our first rational approach to the irrational. Since this is true, it is not surprising to find it becoming of ever increasing importance both to psychiatry and to clinical medicine.

CHAPTER IX

What Is Mental Health?

IN THIS chapter I shall attempt to give a definition of mental health, although it must be admitted that we psychiatrists know more about mental illness than we do about mental health. There are several reasons for this. First, our work brings us constantly face to face with men and women and children who are, as the modern expression has it, maladjusted. Second, mental health is a positive good and does not consist merely in the absence of symptoms of illness, yet it cannot be defined as a fixed and constant condition. In this it is not unlike a state of grace. It is a subtle equilibrium between certain forces which exist within the personality and in the outer world. What some of these forces are and how they interreact upon each other I shall try to show. But let me mention an additional reason why mental health is difficult to define. In the field of psychiatry we have not the kind of accurate statistical data which we possess in the physical sciences. In medicine, for example, we can state pretty accurately what the normal basal metabolic rate should be for a given height, weight, age, and sex. We know the normal pulse rate at rest, the normal blood count, and what deviations from it signify. These examples are familiar enough. They are based on a mass of statistical data. So when a friend says to us: "My doctor gave me a thorough physical examination and I am relieved to say that he found everything perfectly normal," that statement makes sense. But if the same friend said: "Today

I called on my psychiatrist. After an hour's interview he declared that I was perfectly normal. What a relief!" Such a statement might perplex us. If our friend was perfectly normal, why did he go to see a psychiatrist? Why was he relieved to be told he was normal? He must have had some doubt about it himself. Why does he speak of "*my* psychiatrist"? Has he the habit of calling on him? If he had stayed with him two hours, instead of one, perhaps he would not have been found so normal after all. How does a psychiatrist, of all people, know when a man is normal?

Let me digress for a moment and consider the word "normal," so much in use and so highly prized as an attribute. It is the adjective of norm, which derives from the Latin *norma*, meaning a rule. It has the double implication of an authoritative standard, a model, a type, a pattern, and also of a statistically derived mathematical mean or average. There are other instances where such semantic differences lead to confused thinking, but perhaps none more striking than in the field of human behavior, where we use the word "normal" not only in its derivative mathematical sense but to characterize whatever falls within the conventionally accepted range of behavior. A normal man is good and kind and sufficiently aggressive not to let the grass grow under his feet. If he is slothful and gluttonous and given to deception and shady practices, we consider him abnormal. This is largely because such a man does not behave in a conventionally acceptable way.

I once knew a little girl who wrote a cynical fairy story which ended with: "And so they were married and divorced and lived unhappily ever after." Has this story a normal or an abnormal ending? We shall, I think, make better headway in our exploration into mental health if we leave out of consideration such rather rigid and categorical concepts as normal and abnormal and look at mental health always *relatively:* relative to the cultural setting, to the age of the individual, to his social background, and, above all, to the way in which he functions in his work, in his love, in his play, and in his relations with others. If we consider it from this point of view, we shall soon find how few absolute statements we can make. What is illness in one person may be health in another. This should encourage and reassure us.

I will illustrate what I have in mind with a story: James Crawford, a well-known and well-to-do corporation lawyer of the firm of Crawford, Smith, Blankley, Beesley and Everett, left his home as usual in the morning to go to his office. His wife thought him a bit distrait when he said goodbye to her, and instead of eating his usual hearty breakfast he walked out of the house without even his orange juice and coffee. He directed his chauffeur to a neighborhood health food shop where he ordered a bowl of goat's milk. He then dismissed his car and proceeded to walk the five miles to his office. It was a chilly day. On the way he passed a poor-looking man who seemed ill clad. Mr. Crawford took off his overcoat and the double-breasted jacket of his business suit and gave it to the poor man. He passed a "Five and Ten" and bought himself a tin drinking cup. Instead of paying the salesgirl a nickel for it, he gave her a new twenty-dollar bill, which was all that his wallet contained, and he told her to keep the change. After walking a couple of miles, he passed a fashionable shoe store. There was a sign in the window saying, "Clothes Depot—If you have old shoes to dispose of—no matter how worn—leave them here. We will repair them and undertake to send them to the needy people of Europe." Crawford entered the store. He took off his well-polished brogues and handed them to an amazed clerk, saying that he could wear them no longer because they were made of calfskin. He trudged the rest of the way to his office in stocking feet. When he arrived at his office on Wall Street, he did not enter the revolving door. Instead he sat down on the pavement with his legs crossed in as near the Buddha position as his stiff joints and corpulent abdomen would permit. He held the empty tin cup in his hand and sat silently with head bowed, contemplating the lowest button of his waistcoat. At about five o'clock when the subway rush hour began, a policeman came along. He tapped Mr. Crawford lightly on the sole of a stockinged foot, through which his dirty bare toes now projected, and told him to move along. Mr. Crawford looked up as from a revery. He tried to make the policeman understand that he had been in deep meditation, that for the first time in his life he was in communion with God, that he had reached a state of inner harmony and peace which he had never before even aspired to. But the policeman was obdurate, and he said to one of the gaping group of bystanders, "He's psycho all right, I guess I'll have to take him to Bellevue." His wife was sent for. She was terribly distressed. He was quite out of contact. He was not in the least concerned with his daughter's coming-out party which was to take place two days later, or with the case of the *Consolidated Aero-Dynamics Company* v. *The People of the State of New York*, which was on the calendar of the Appellate Division for the following week and in which there were millions of dollars of stockholders' money involved, with a proportionately large fee for his firm. The next day he was moved to an expensive private mental hospital where two special nurses were engaged for him. As he had refused to go of his own accord, protesting that he had at last found the way to truth and serenity, he had to be legally certified by two sympathetic but stubborn psychiatrists. The diagnosis was "catatonic schizophrenia in the setting of the involutional period." The prognosis was "guarded."

Suppose that Crawford's name had been Swamarami, and his skin not sallow white but a rich brown, and that he had taken off his jeweled turban and his silk robes and seated himself under a banyan tree; who would have been considered abnormal, the holy man or the constable who had arrested him?

Here, then, is our first important variable: the cultural setting in which the individual exists. And accordingly this is our first proposition: *Mental health consists in a certain degree of conformity with the cultural patterns of the community.*

Let me give a few more brief examples: A Yankee or a Yorkshire farmer who sold his daughter in marriage in exchange for a prize bull would be guilty of a callousness and an inhumanity so at variance with the mores of his group that his mental health would certainly be questioned. But an African tribesman, perhaps no less devoted to his daughter, might receive congratulations for having driven a shrewd bargain.

A Parisian academician could not build a shrine to his ancestors and lay dishes of burning crêpes suzette and bottles of vintage wine on the altar without being justly suspected of mental unbalance. But there are parts of the world where such practices are not only usual, but he who does not indulge in them might be looked at askance as irreligious and irreverent.

A friend of mine, recently returned from China, was shown while there a notice in the local newspaper of a small town, which, freely translated, ran this way: "Mr. Weng Fu, the well-known silk merchant, has eloped with his serving maid. This is unfortunate. We had always believed that he lived in peace and contentment with his concubine."

The number of wives we have and the number of mistresses and whether they are overtly acknowledged or clandestine is, to be sure, a matter of custom and mores, but whoever deviates too brazenly from the legal and cultural standard of his group will be looked upon as perverse or psychopathic.

Group standards to which we must conform in order to be considered in sound mental health need not, of course, be national, racial, or religious ones. Much smaller aggregates of people set up theirs, too, and expect conformity. The modern American college youth has practically discarded the hat as an article of clothing, but he may not yet cross the campus to go to his classes barefooted or without his trousers, without being thought more than eccentric. In my day at college we wore hats because we wore hats, and only a few long-haired poets could have gone without them. Society has always made allowances for the rich, the powerful, the genius, and the artist, who are permitted to deviate from standard behavior in far greater degree than are ordinary people.

This criterion of mental health, namely, conformity with the cultural patterns of the community, which I have submitted as my first proposition, may seem both conventional and superficial, but I think that you will realize from some of the examples that I have given that it is not one to be underestimated.

Let me now proceed to my second proposition, so closely related to the first one. It is this: *Our feelings, thoughts, and acts must exhibit a certain appropriateness.* In other words, they must correspond in greater or less degree not only to group standards but to an outer reality. Here, again, I am treading on dangerous ground, because I should not care to be seduced into a definition of reality. Instead I will turn, once more, to the use of example.

Miss Brown, a middle-aged but energetic and efficient woman, has for many years been engaged as a bookkeeper-stenographer in a certain business house. She is one of its most valued and respected employees, distinguished for her loyalty, her extraordinary attention to detail, and her complete reliability. Although a somewhat tense and sensitive person, she has always enjoyed good but distant relationships with her fellow-workers. For her employer no amount of trouble and extra work was too much for her. She was especially proud of her attendance record and of the fact that for over ten years she had not missed a day's work because of ill health. She began, however, to have trouble with an old wisdom tooth, which finally had to be extracted. The actual operation was a trivial one, done under a local anesthetic. The tooth was not impacted and its removal caused no great amount of pain. But Miss Brown was apprehensive about the extraction, and after it was over she felt exhausted and tearful and was constantly preoccupied with the episode. She would go to the mirror several times a day and scrutinize, as best she could, the place where the tooth had been. Her appetite fell off, and she found it more and more difficult to concentrate on her work. Even reading the daily paper seemed to require a greater intellectual effort than she could muster.

As the company's books were about to be examined by the accountants, Miss Brown became more and more agitated. She finally was convinced that she had falsified them, that she would be found out and sent to jail. She thought that her boss, who had always been so appreciative and encouraging, was suddenly hostile and critical because he knew what she had done, and she believed that the new elevator man was actually a detective put there to spy upon her.

I need hardly dwell on the inappropriateness of Miss Brown's mood and thinking, on how she overreacted to a rather slight trauma, the tooth extraction, which, however, had some inner meaning for her far beyond its real one. Her need to distort reality, to make of herself a criminal, which she was not, and to make enemies of her friends and associates is part of this same process that we call "paranoid projection." When carried to this extreme, it is evidence of rather severe mental illness. In Miss Brown's case one can see the precursors of such illness in the rigidity of her personality, in her single-tracked existence, and in her sensitiveness. The tooth extraction simply upset the unstable equilibrium of her adjustment to life.

I could give many less extreme examples of inappropriate thoughts and feelings which are pointers to mental ill health, among them, unaccountable fears and phobias, bizarre and unwelcome obsessive thoughts, animosities and prejudices based on subjective feelings with little relation to fact. It is one thing to freeze in a paroxysm of terror with the hot breath of a wounded tiger on our heels but quite a different thing to experience the same feelings, for no known reason, while walking on the street.

In the area of the emotions, appropriateness is again largely a matter of common sense and convention. If a person feels very different from the way others would feel under similar circumstances, his feelings will be looked upon as inappropriate.

With acts we have somewhat more objective criteria. An appropriate act must be directed toward a goal, and the means used to accomplish it must be adapted to the end. We cannot expect to catch moonbeams in a butterfly net and be thought sane. A person in a state of mental health will direct his acts toward the achievement of a realizable goal, no matter how remote, and the possession of such a goal is one criterion for judging whether his acts are healthy ones or not. This, then, I should like to submit as my third proposition: *That our acts must be directed toward a realizable goal, however remote, and that the means we employ must be adapted toward achieving the goal.* A very practical, prosaic, and pedestrian proposition, you will say. Does the list of the healthy-minded include only cobblers, street cleaners, and locomotive engineers, men whose activities are obviously goal-directed? What about visionaries, reformers, prophets, and poets? I should certainly not exclude them, provided that their dreams are in some manner, however distantly, translatable into realities. But if a man says: "I want to save the world by radium" and has no notion of what he means, either by saving the world or of how it can be done with the use of radium, then I think his mental health may be questioned.

Again, if a man has no goal, but wanders hither and yon —driven by some inner restless urge that he does not understand—such a man is probably not mentally healthy. Here is an example: It is a verbatim report, taken from a book of autobiographies written for the twenty-fifth class reunion of one of our famous eastern universities. This is what the alumnus, then presumably a man of forty-five, says of himself:

> For fifteen years I worked in factories, stores, and offices at a minimum wage. Since then I have worked on farms. In May, I walked from Boston into Vermont, staying on one farm five months. In December, I walked to Manhattan. I either played or worked at being a Bowery bum all winter. The nearest New York City could come to affording me a job was tending fire for my lodging in a little hotel. In May and June, a year later, I made my way, with no money, over the highways to ten miles west of Chicago. I then turned back to near Cleveland, Ohio.

One wonders what impulses motivated him, what goal he was seeking, what satisfaction he obtained, other than the primitive one of survival. Without knowing more about him we cannot say. But his story seems a kind of paradigm of modern man turned loose in a world too big, too complicated, and utterly defeating. He is unable either to bend his environment to his needs or to adjust his needs to his environment. And so his life consists of a series of startings and stoppings and of aimless backtracking adding up to nothing and contributing to no one's good.

Does this mean that, in order to be mentally healthy, our aims must be creative ones and must contribute to the good of society? Yes, I believe so. Hitler had his goals—all too nearly realized—and yet who can doubt from his quixotic nature, mystical and superstitious, and from the all-inclusiveness of the hatred and destruction that inspired him, that he was essentially psychopathic?

This, then, is our fourth proposition of mental health: *That not only must we possess realizable goals, but they must be constructive ones, related to social good.* I do not mean this in any highfalutin way. Socially constructive goals may include the most menial occupations, provided that they contribute to communal living. They do not include the career of the gambler, the wastrel, the criminal, and the parasite. In our society these occupations are not compatible with our conception of mental health. You will see, then, that it is impossible to divorce concepts of mental health from ethical ones. This I hold to be true in spite of the pronouncements of certain parochial pundits, who choose to see an antithesis between psychiatry and religion. In so far as both are concerned with problems of good and evil, psychiatry and religion are not antithetical. It is not, however, the task of psychiatry to devise ethical systems but rather to recognize their validity and to acknowledge that in civilized man a state of mental health is not possible when they are disregarded.

These four propositions that I have laid down should not be accepted in any absolute sense. They are at best rough approximations. Together they form a kind of coarse screen through which we can separate certain aspects of mental illness from mental health. Undoubtedly, each proposition needs to be qualified. For example, of the first one we might say with equal truth that under some circumstances nonconformity with the cultural patterns of the community is evidence of health rather than of illness. The man who stands alone against the rabble, who is an innovator or even a revolutionary, is frequently healthier than those who oppose him.

Similarly, the feelings and acts of the poet, the visionary, the creative genius, are often at great variance with those of more ordinary people. It would be foolish and meaningless to diagnose those, on any such grounds, as mentally ill. Again, the goals of some few may be far beyond our comprehension and may consist primarily in an effort toward self-development and self-fulfilment. Such goals perhaps appear unrelated to social good, and yet those who possess them and pursue them may be eminently sound.

Even with these qualifications the four propositions seem to me useful and based on experience and sound sense. As I have said, they help us sort out, in an approximate way, those who are seriously disturbed from those who are relatively well adjusted.

The task of psychiatry is no longer what it once was, to care only for the insane or what today we call "psychotics." Once the psychiatrist functioned principally as an alienist whose chief job was to examine the mentally sick, declare them insane, and commit them to what were called in the blunt and cruel language of the past, lunatic asylums—a term reminiscent of Hogarth's Bedlam—where they received custodial, if any, care. It has become clear, however, that even the major psychoses differ only quantitatively from disturbances far less malignant, and resemble in many ways patterns which exist in all of us. True, the psychoses represent a gross breakdown in the machine which sometimes makes it impossible for it to function because of memory defects, extreme disturbances of mood, delusions, hallucinations, and other deviations which a layman would recognize as abnormal. We have been taught to distinguish between these severe psychotic reactions and less malignant neurotic ones by the test of the patient's adjustment to reality. Does he distort reality, misinterpret it, and live in a world of his own fanciful creation? Though it is true that such a test is a roughly useful one, it would be a far cry from the truth to say that the most normal and healthy of us does not constantly need to deny reality. But we do not do so in an all-out way. We do not run out on it altogether as some psychotics do. Reality is often a cold and unpalatable dish. Through our fantasy and creative imaginations we provide ourselves with more succulent fare. The capacity to do this may be an important one in the maintenance of mental health, which is a feat rather like tightrope walking, achieved not by assuming a rigid stance on the wire but by a swift and subtle process of constantly losing balance and recapturing it.

The war showed us very clearly that under circumstances of constant exposure to bombardment, fatigue, hunger, and above all to the inner moral conflict between the desire to escape into safety and the command to stand firm, breakdowns occurred which resembled almost exactly some of those seen in the major psychoses. In most instances the acute disturbance subsided rather quickly upon removal from danger, but the task of rehabilitation always required understanding and dealing with certain inner forces of the individual.

From what I have just been saying it may be concluded that susceptibility to mental illness is as widespread in the community as susceptibility to measles. In other words, it is universal. This has both its encouraging and its disquieting aspects—encouraging because we now know that even sweeping and profound disturbances are not necessarily irreversible ones and that the field of prevention is open before us; disquieting because it puts the burden of maintaining mental health squarely up to all of us. Understanding its nature is, therefore, no mere academic and intellectual pastime. It is essential to the primary needs of any society.

You will probably have observed that every time I have made a positive statement about what mental health is, I have had, at once, to qualify the statement. I will go on a little longer with this approach. Like the golfer who addresses the ball with a few preliminary swings before he makes his final drive, I will continue trying to improve my stance. Here, then, is a fifth proposition to think about. It is this: *That the maintenance of mental health depends upon the capacity for getting pleasure and satisfaction from what we experience.* Without this, no conformity, no appropriateness, no purpose, and no achievement will suffice. If in our relations with others, in our work, in our love, in the functions of our bodies, we cannot get pleasure and satisfaction, it is hard to conceive that we can enjoy mental health. Indeed, if for some reason we cannot find such satisfactions, we are all prone to exploit substitute ones and to replace pleasure with pain and suffering. This is the reverse of mental health—the all-too-prevalent neurotic invalidism of modern life.

But pleasure is not for the asking. There are many situations in life when we are denied it, when what we most urgently want and need we cannot have. This is often a supreme test of mental health, the ability to withstand frustration and denial. Each one of us has a stress tolerance beyond which he cannot be tried. For some the limit is quickly reached, though within the area of their capacities they may function exceedingly well. A close corollary to this fifth proposition is this: That we must not only derive pleasure and satisfaction from what we experience but that *life must be lived with energy, zest, and spontaneity*. There are many circumstances, to be sure, which deny us pleasure, which give us the opposite of satisfaction, and there is much drudgery and travail in everyone's existence. If we expect to go bouncing and bubbling through life, we are childish and foolish. But I think it is true that the healthy man comes back to these positive attitudes as naturally as the sunflower turns toward the sun.

This last proposition, together with the others, will serve to screen out those neurotically disturbed persons about whose difficulties we have in the last fifty years acquired a great deal of useful knowledge. What passes through the sieve is all the rest of us—people neither psychotic nor suffering from serious psychoneuroses, who have potentialities for mental illness as well as for mental health, depending upon the interaction of certain forces within us and in the world around us.

If we try to define this group more closely or characterize it, we shall not succeed too well. Attempts to do so have not been conspicuously fruitful. We have, as yet, no satisfactory definition of a normal mind. The best we can do is to approximate one by the use of such abstractions as efficiency. Or we can try to exemplify it by enumerating names of great men who have exhibited unusual intellectual vigor and creative genius. But surely such men as Leonardo da Vinci, Napoleon, Goethe, or Abraham Lincoln are not normal in any sense of "standard" or "average." Each, moreover, exhibited in his life symptoms such as depression, anxiety, and hypochondriasis. Whether they would have been greater or less great without these disabilities, who can say? According to the distinguished English psychoanalyst, Ernest Jones, "the nearest attainable criterion of normality is fearlessness," and by this he means not merely courage but the absence of anxiety and "the willing or even joyful acceptance of life, with all its visitations and chances, that distinguishes the free personality of one who is master of himself." Such an ideal construction, although it has its beauty, is perhaps unattainable. I doubt very much whether any person of even as much as average intelligence can live in this world without some anxiety—however concealed it may be.

If we dip our pitcher into the well of the poet, the philosopher, and the saint, we will come up with the same clear water. In his *Testament of Beauty*, Robert Bridges said: "Our stability is but balance and wisdom lies in the masterful administration of the Unseen."

It is the function of poets to have visions and, like the man in the crow's-nest, to descry a landfall. But the scientist's place is in the engine-room. He is concerned with mechanisms, with an inquiry into how things work. It is not enough for him to catch a glimpse of perfection and to say, "This is mental health," without an exploration into how it is achieved.

I stated before that the knowledge we have won in the last fifty years has given us insight into psychoneurotic illness. It has also given us insight into the dynamics of personality. By this term we mean those interacting forces of which the resultant is the character of the individual. What some of these forces are and where they exist was discussed in the chapter on "Psychoanalysis."

The relationship of the unconscious to the conscious may be compared to a hydroelectric system, consisting of a reservoir, a dam, and a spillway. The reservoir represents the unconscious forces of the id, the dam the powers of repression of the superego, and the spillway the active outwardly directed conscious life of the ego. If the reservoir pours over the dam, the individual is flooded with disorganized, primitive, often undirected thoughts and feelings. These, then, cannot be made to conform to the cultural patterns of the group in which we live. They lack appropriateness, and because of the rush of the waters of the unconscious, our acts will be haphazard and not goal-directed, nor can they be put to the service of society. None of the first four propositions for mental health, which I laid down at the beginning of this chapter, will be fulfilled. On the other hand, if the dam is too high and only a trickle of water finds an outlet into the spillway, there will be no energy, no drive, and no pleasure in life. The fifth proposition, namely, the one relating to the capacity for obtaining pleasure and satisfaction, will not be taken into account. This is what happened to poor Miss Brown, the bookkeeper-secretary whose constrained and constricted manner of living resulted in a serious depression. But if the reservoir pours a steady stream into the spillway, then life can move forward with a zest and our primitive drives can be channeled into effective, pleasurable, and satisfactory living. But, again, if in the outer world insurmountable difficulties and obstacles arise, if the spillway is blocked, the system may back up, and the reservoir, finding no outlet, will overflow the dam.

A clearer understanding of how this machine operates may be gained by analogy with the workings of the body. In the middle of the last century the great French physiologist, Claude Bernard, asserted that the constancy of the internal environment of the body is the condition of free and independent life. To use his own words: "There is an arrangement in the living being, a kind of regulated activity, which must never be neglected, because it is in truth the most striking characteristic of living beings." This regulated activity was given the name "homeostasis" by my own revered teacher, the late Professor Walter B. Cannon. The relative uniformity of blood sugar, or body temperature, for example, and the slight alkalinity of the blood may be regarded as samples of the effects of nice devices at work in the organism. A steady state is maintained because any tendency toward change is automatically met by corrective reactions. If, for example, we hold our breath, carbon dioxide piles up in the blood, making it more acid. This stimulates the respiratory center to make us breathe deeply. We thereupon blow off carbon dioxide. The blood is restored to its normal alkalinity and respirations return to their normal depth and frequency. Another familiar analogy is the thermostatic control of room temperature. When the temperature falls, the oil-burner motor starts and steam comes up in the radiator until the temperature rises to a constant level, when the oil-burner stops and the radiator cools off.

We can assume that in the maintenance of mental and emotional health some such self-regulatory processes are at work. These entail a compensatory and reciprocal shift in the various forces of the mind. Take, for example, the situation of a young boy at adolescence whose sexual needs and strivings are mounting in intensity. In other words, the demands of the id are making themselves felt not only in bodily sensations but perhaps by giving rise to fantasies and images which still more excite his desires. But these demands are met by strong dictates from his conscience or superego which prohibits any direct expression of his sexual wishes. The ego is then faced with this conflict. In the meanwhile society, which erects the barriers against sexual gratification in adolescents, also does its best to seduce and stimulate them with aphrodisiac posters, advertisements, and movies. What will happen to the boy? He may turn to religion as adolescents often do and strengthen the forces of suppression and thus appear to resolve his conflict. He may, if the mores of his cultural group permit, simply overcome his scruples and find some source of gratification in the outer world. He may find substitute gratifications in athletic pursuits. Or the result may be an unstable balance of forces. The boy will then become more and more tense. He will probably develop difficulties in concentrating on his school work and may indeed become delinquent.

Or, again, consider what changes are required in the superego of a young lad who has been brought up in a peace-loving family and who from early childhood has had a strict religious and moral upbringing, when he is trained and ordered to thrust a bayonet into the belly of an adversary. I have had many young soldiers tell me of this experience and how they felt, not when they drove the bayonet in, but when they pulled it out and when they saw what they had done. But feelings of loyalty to one's country and outfit, the reward of a battle star, and the hope to get it all over with and go home take precedence over the prohibitions against killing, and the soldier can go about his job in a business-like way. If he cannot, he will either be bayoneted himself or be returned as a psychiatric casualty because of a conflict that he cannot resolve.

These examples are two of many one could give to illustrate the subtle shift of forces that takes place automatically. The first, that of the boy with the mounting sexual tension, was chosen because the changes introduced began within the developing organism; the second example, of the soldier, was chosen because here the organism found itself in a new environment and had to change in order to survive.

It must be evident that the adaptive capacity of the individual is a variable one, varying not only at different times of his life but in response to a constantly altering environment. Why some people are able to make quick and necessary internal shifts and others are not is still far from clear. We say that it depends in part upon their state of maturity. If they carry over into adult life the undifferentiated reaction patterns of their infancy, they will lack the necessary versatility and resourcefulness to measure up to the demands of reality. A baby cannot earn his living, marry, raise children, and take a responsible part in the community, and yet many adults in spite of physiological maturity remain essentially infantile.

Perhaps I have made it appear that keeping one's mental health is a pretty tricky business. But, fortunately, the processes that I have been describing take place, for the most part, automatically. We are made of pretty tough materials and can stand a good deal of kicking around. Most of us, however, in one way or another, get enough of it. It is important that we do not kick ourselves around, that we take a relaxed, friendly, humorous attitude toward ourselves. We cannot live our lives by will-power alone. Although self-discipline is an excellent thing, if we constantly drive the machine in ways it is not set to go, it will finally fail. The still small voice of conscience may be the basis of our morality, but remember, we were not born with all of it. It was put there not only by our parents, whom we may revere, but also often by ignorant nursegirls and by the unenlightened mores of a narrow and bigoted community. A constantly vigilant sense of guilt leads more often to vice than it does to virtue.

It is a good thing to wrestle with one's soul for the right. But it is not a good thing to be grimly ascetic with one's self or to deny one's self healthy and positive pleasures. If we pursue such a course with the mistaken notion that it is a virtuous one, the chances are that we will end by inflicting pain on others as well as on ourselves. A healthy democratic society depends upon an attitude of tolerance among its citizens. To be tolerant of others, we must first of all be tolerant toward ourselves. That is often difficult, but I believe that it is a first and necessary step toward mental health.

CHAPTER X

On Choosing a Mate

It is not surprising just now when the divorce rate is mounting and when young couples and others are having a hard time finding a roof over their heads and when so many brides are wage-earners that the difficulties of marriage are being widely discussed. Men and women concerned with the stability of family life in America have written and talked much on this subject and considered it from many angles—sociological, religious, psychological, and others. Marriage-counseling services are established in many cities to give young people advice and help in facing their problems. In spite of all this thought and activity there is much still that needs to be understood and there are many points of difference.

Here, for example, is what a Catholic priest said, as reported in a recent edition of the *New York Evening Sun:* "A marriage based on love alone is doomed. People in love are the worst possible ones to pick mates objectively. The formula for successful marriage is comprised of four *M's*—Mind, Money, Manners and Morals." Now I have no quarrel with the holy father. Indeed, I am much interested in the order of his specifications. Nor have I any fault to find with mind, money, manners, or morals, especially in a wife; but I am skeptical of all formulas that propose to govern human behavior, and I do not see how a highly subjective relationship can be assessed entirely objectively as if, for example, one were buying a new car. In any event, perhaps it would be wiser to ask the man who owns one, so to speak, rather than to take the advice of a person whose profession forbids him even to learn to drive.

Whatever psychiatrists or priests may think of the pleasures or perils of falling in love, the phenomenon seems to be here to stay as a basis for most modern marriages. And nothing that we say about it will banish it or change materially what has become a familiar part of our cultural pattern. Of course, it was not always so. It may not always be so. There are parts of the world today where marriages are arranged for reasons of status, security, or business, and where the love of the two principals is a nonexistent or negligible factor in the contract.

If you will go back a few generations to the New England of some of your forebears, you may have to admit that your Hepzibahs and Mirandas married their Elijahs and Hezekiahs not so much in the heat of romantic emotion but because in Colonial New England the Puritans often arranged marriages for their children with an eye on money and social position. The prospective son-in-law had to be God-fearing and prudent, of course, but he also had to be of the same kind of people. If he came from a well-feathered nest, he was the better catch. The young people were seldom alone or unchaperoned. Perhaps he waited for her outside the church and walked her to her door. Perhaps he stole a kiss, against blushes and halfhearted protests, which were part of the stereotyped behavior of the time. Perhaps he could take her for a sleigh ride. And then finally he would ask her father for her hand, and the old man would do some quick figuring and perhaps give his blessing; or perhaps not. The young girl's fate was pretty much in the hands of her parents, who had had a similar upbringing themselves. And sometimes the parents rejoiced greatly over their good fortune. As Groucho Marx put it: "When my wife and I were married, you never saw a happier couple—than her parents."

Compare this with a modern scene: Joan comes home from the office. Her father is in the living room reading the evening paper. She kisses him on the top of his bald head with a "Hi, Pop." Then she says: "How about I should marry Jack?" Her father is deep in baseball scores or stock quotations. What Joan has said to him has hardly registered. Joan finally explodes: "Well, Dad, aren't you going to say anything? After all!" Then Dad comes to. He looks at her with strange eyes. She has always been his pet. He wants her to be happy. He knows she is a good clean girl. I have found that all fathers seem to know that about their own daughters. He is getting sentimental. There are tears in his eyes, and he says: "Are you in love with him, darling?" Joan says: "I guess so—but sometimes I think I don't know what love really is. Anyway I know I can't do without him." And that is that.

Jack has to be honest. He must not have had a jail record. Joan's father probably hopes that the boy is a Protestant and a Republican. He could come from the other side of the tracks. He could be a Catholic. He could even be Jewish—though preferably not, since that might make for embarrassment and great difficulties. He could not be colored. But the important thing is that the two young people are very much in love with each other.

Toward the differentiation between what we might, for the moment, call real love and neurotic love a psychiatrist has a special contribution to make; and this for several reasons. First of all, the nature of his work brings him into contact, sometimes daily contact, with people who talk to him more or less freely about the most intimate part of their lives. He sees men and women falling in love and out of love. He recognizes that there is no more fundamental force in the human mind than the craving for love. He is aware of the many forms of expression that this craving may take. Dependence on others, demand for praise and recognition, ambition, an insatiable hunger for superiority or fame or wealth—all of these may represent more or less successful vicarious attempts at being loved. The craving seeks satisfaction in sexual love and infatuation. Some try to satisfy it by overeating or by excessive drinking. It may be turned toward the opposite sex or toward the same sex or toward the person himself.

The psychiatrist recognizes, moreover, that part of this need to be loved is a kind of anachronism, originating in the helplessness of childhood when protective parental care is the essential condition of survival. But often it persists into adulthood, when ideally it should have been replaced by self-reliance, self-confidence, and the capacity to form tender and enduring attachments. This infantile love is neither tender nor enduring. It cannot be. It is desperate, clinging, predatory, manipulative, and cares more about its own feelings than about the other person. It is often closely allied to feelings of hate.

If the psychiatrist had any doubts about the traces of this kind of love, which in greater or less degree survive in all of us, they would be quickly dispelled in the process of psychoanalytic treatment, because there he will have the opportunity of observing in the so-called "transference" relationship the very phenomenon which I have been discussing and, moreover, in a kind of pure form. In the course of psychoanalytic treatment patients usually lose the practical, realistic attitude of an intelligent human being seeking cure of an illness. Instead they shift to a neurotic pattern in which childish and emotional features predominate. They distort the image of the analyst into a god or sometimes a devil; they demand gratification from him with imperiousness. They expect him somehow to fulfil all their needs, to satisfy all their cravings. They fly in the face of reality and try to convert the relationship into anything but the professional one it must remain.

The psychiatrist recognizes that he is being forced into a role, that his patient is unconsciously identifying him with someone out of the past with whom he has previously played this old game of love and hate. But the patient is loath to see, often cannot see for a long time, the true nature of his attachment. It feels to him like love. But it is not love in any mature and adult sense. It lacks mutuality and love must be mutual. It lacks tender concern with the needs of the other and does not take into account the realities of his life. It arrives at no goal. It is concerned with subjective emotions and the excitement that they invoke. It is not what we call an object relationship. It is not "other-person-centered."

And yet, this kind of transference love which we psychiatrists see developing in our consulting rooms and which with patience and steadiness of purpose we try to dissolve is quite analogous to the neurotic love on which many marriages are based. "I want a girl just like the girl that married dear old Dad." "You remind me of my Mother when Mother was a girl like you." Those of you who listen to the Hit Parade could, I am sure, supply me with many more recent titles: all the baby-doll, sugar-candy, love-in-a-cottage, you-hoo and me-hee songs that represent mass-medium love.

Now I am not suggesting that young men and women should sing songs of social significance to each other, but the wild goose knows more about marriage than many of these human goslings. She builds her nest, sits on her eggs, stays there, helps her fledglings. And the gander does his turn by standing guard. And, what's more, they are said by some to be monogamous.

Nor am I suggesting that we emulate wild fowl or that man's romantic proclivities and his tendency to idealize the object of his love are not ennobling emotions. There is surely a fine line between love that is only a grand and glorious feeling and love that leads to a deep understanding and to the joy that comes from sharing hopes and experiences and even routine jobs. Have we of the older generation anything to tell younger people to help them differentiate between those loves? Will they listen to us if we have? If they are sufficiently healthy, perhaps they will not need our advice, and, on the other hand, if they are sufficiently neurotic, they will not take it.

When I was at Harvard College, Dean Le Baron Russell Briggs—that wonderful, humorous, and beloved figure—read a story to every entering Freshman class. It was a tale of a fine young Boston boy who was engaged to a member of the Sewing Circle or of the Vincent Club; but he strayed off Brattle Street one night and had his fling. So his fiancée threw him over, and the last lines I remember well, though it is now forty-two years since I heard them: "Couldn't you have waited for me, Dick?" she said. Can you imagine the catcalls and whistles that such a simple tale would elicit from any Freshman class today?

The change in our mores was not brought about by a man named Kinsey and his popular book on the sexual life of the savages. In those days Kinsey probably would have been tarred and feathered and run out of town, instead of being recognized as an important contributor to scientific knowledge. The change has come—gradually at first and now perhaps accelerating—as an accompaniment of certain social and economic trends in our environment. A few of the more important ones might be mentioned: the shift of populations toward large urban centers, and with this the lessening of the influence and control of the community on the individual, so that each man is for himself, so to speak, and feels that he can do what he likes. And each woman too. Women have been emancipated, as we say, though we seldom ask, emancipated from what or for what. Family ties have loosened;

parents have lost authority and are no longer the final arbiters of their children's fate. Religious observances in most homes have declined almost to the vanishing point. "The trend in the United States," to quote Professor E. W. Burgess, "has been away from the conception of marriage as a contract sanctioned by law and community pressure toward that of an interpersonal relation expressive of companionship."

This has put a great burden on our young people. When they choose a mate, they are choosing a companion for life, one they like to be with both out of bed and in bed. They are not choosing a household drudge or a helpmeet or a perfect son-in-law for their parents. How are they to recognize such a companion when they see him? There are no easy rules to guide them. It takes experience and more sense than can be expected of most young people.

In our practical and empirical age youth has adopted the experimental method. In coeducational schools they first look each other over. At parties they have long since abandoned the dance card and the little gold pencil and have substituted cutting-in, which affords the maximum number of contacts in the shortest possible time. The successful girl is the one who hardly knows with whom she is dancing before she is dancing with another.

"Dating" begins early in the middle teens. Burgess calls it "one of the great social innovations of our time." No one invented it. It arose as an adaptation to the new needs of young people. It extends their experience and gives boys and girls a chance to get to know each other. You try one date and then another, but you are already on the still hunt for the perfect companion. In some of our large western state universities the boys in fraternity houses keep elaborate card-index systems of the coeds, and one could find such an entry as this: "Susie Jones is a dumb cluck. Won't even neck." There is a difference, none too subtle, between necking and petting. The dividing line is the collarbone. Standards vary. The girl who does nothing gets a bad mark, and so–sometimes–does the girl who does everything. The middle ground seems the most coveted. As an old lady whom I know put it: "Why they talk about anything! But they don't talk about anything else."

Dating sometimes leads to "going with" a person–a more concentrated but yet not exclusive relationship. You are still at liberty to date others. And then, if things look promising, you "go steady," which need not necessarily mean love but it implies a strong attachment and one which voluntarily limits the freedom of the couple. They have renounced dating others. Only then do they arrive at a kind of "private understanding" with a mutual avowal of love. This is the final trial heat before the formal engagement. It has the advantage that it can be terminated without embarrassment. By the time that they become formally engaged, the young couple have had an opportunity to get to know each other. The intensity of their first romantic love may indeed have abated somewhat. He may have seen her with a boil on the end of her nose and she him when he was unshaven and grumpy. Even after the engagement is announced, there is often a further delay of a year or more before marriage. This has its advantages and disadvantages. It is a further test of their maturity, of their ability to tolerate a certain kind of frustration, but it also puts off the reality of a consistently close relationship. Naturally enough the engagement period is nowadays often one of sexual intimacy. Whether this is a good or a bad thing, I will leave to you to decide. But from a professional point of view I can say that unwanted pregnancies are bad and that abortions may be rather disastrous for young girls.

I have reviewed these progressive stages, from cutting-in at dances and dating to final engagement, simply to show you how young people have more or less automatically reacted to the changes in marriage that have resulted from recent social and economic trends in our culture. It would be foolish to call them good or bad. They are forces that are with us and to which we must adapt. No sentimental or nostalgic longing for the good old days will reverse these forces, and there is no assurance that the good old days were really so good.

It is true that in Puritan New England, for example, divorce was almost unknown, but that does not prove that marriages were happier then or more creative than they are today. To state, as the Catholic priest did, whom I quoted at the beginning of this chapter, that "a marriage based on love alone is doomed" seems to me an illogical *non sequitur*. It would be more to the point to say that in 1912 the divorce rate was one in ten; in 1940, one in five; in 1946, one in three or four; and, if the present rate continues, by 1950 two out of every three marriages will end in divorce. If there is such a high incidence of doom in modern marriages, is it sound to attribute that unhappy fact to their being based on love alone? I think not. In fact, I am more inclined to the view of that worldly wise gentleman, Ben Franklin, who I believe said, "When there is marriage without love, there will be love without marriage." Marriages today are held together by love and mutual respect and consent, not by outward pressure; and when love vanishes, or is replaced, as it so easily can be, by hatred, they fall apart.

The question for us to try to answer is, why does love vanish, why does it turn to indifference or cruelty or hatred? Why is it apparently so difficult for us to form tender and enduring attachments? I hope that you will not require that I define love. That is a job for the poet.

I use the word "love" not only to include strong mutual physical attraction but to signify the thought of cherishing another, of caring greatly about his welfare. Now this is an ideal difficult to achieve but worth striving for and worth certain sacrifices, because it holds out the greatest promise of personal fulfilment. And when it is approximated, even if not fully achieved, the good from it spreads out and touches the lives of many others.

If we demand the impossible from such a relationship, of course, we will meet disappointment. Nobody but an idiot would hope for perfect and constant happiness in a world such as this. Passing happy and even ecstatic moments, yes, perhaps; but comfort we can expect, and understanding and the feeling that you count enormously in another's life and that what you do and strive for is important to your mate.

In other words, we should not expect constant and perfect love in an imperfect world. But the foundation on which the relationship is built must be firm and be able to withstand moderately strong winds of difference and discord. In the midst of all the forces that impinge on a married couple there must emerge two separate individuals who walk together toward some kind of common goal, be it the rearing of their children or the comfort and respect they give each other or their desire to take part, together, in the life of the community. If they enter into competition with each other, and even with their children, for dependent care, a tension is set up in the relationship which it sometimes cannot endure.

The greatest single enemy of success in marriage is the neurotic disturbance of one or both partners. Now it is as difficult to define a neurosis as it is to define love. As I have used the word loving to be equivalent with the idea of cherishing, I use the concept of neurosis to be equivalent to the idea of emotional immaturity. I know that this is an overworked and not very satisfactory definition. It is a state in which certain ill-adapted modes of behavior and attitudes surviving from childhood seek outlets and satisfactions in situations, especially in relationship with others, that can never fulfil these infantile requirements. Perhaps this could be put somewhat more simply by saying that as children we crave pleasure and we need to be taken care of by our parents and we are accustomed to being the center of their attention. It takes a long time to grow up emotionally, to reach a point when we are mature enough to be parents, to be at the giving, rather than at the receiving, end, and to contribute not only to the support and care of our children but to the good of the community.

Many of these childish attitudes and expectations prevail, however. When they run counter to the realities of life, the result is conflict, tension, often undue guilt, aggression, and anxiety, which are among the symptoms of neurotic disorder. A great many defensive measures are then mobilized against these reactions. One of the commonest is to blame the marital partner for our own failures and disappointments, and a second is to attribute to the other person our own defects. Marriage usually does not cure neurotic illness; neither does having babies. The new demands and new responsibilities often make things worse, rather than better. Neurotic disturbance more than anything else interferes with the formation of permanent tender attachments. The love that exists under such circumstances is too tinctured with hate and the hate is too intolerable.

Marriages that come to grief are often contracted for neurotic reasons. One partner is drawn to the other with the hope that by some magic he will imbibe the other's virtues and somehow compensate for his own defects. The clinging vine chooses the strong man, but she may be frightened and intimidated by his strength or not find the support that her childish dependence demands. Or the weak, indecisive man picks a motherly, secure paragon of a woman who does indeed give him support but renders him weaker in the process. There are innumerable combinations of personalities, but without some flexibility and adaptability it is unlikely that they will work together very well. When reactions are too stereotyped because of the dominance of childish traits, the chances of success in marriage are greatly reduced. This does not mean that the resort to childish pleasures has no place in the life of an adult. On the contrary, to be able to indulge them, at times, is essential to health and to happy love relations. But to choose a mate wisely, we must, first of all, be able to accept and live in the real world.

CHAPTER XI

Why the Professor Fell Out of Bed

HEALTH and happiness are relative conceptions. They are somewhat ill-defined and subjective abstractions. We know, and no one else does, when we feel healthy and happy. Our doctor may tell us that everything is perfect: that our weight, pulse rate, metabolism, electrocardiogram, reflexes, blood count, excretions, etc., are all normal, and yet we may suffer from headaches, sleeplessness, a general feeling of lassitude, apathy, and discouragement. Or we may be the president of the largest savings bank in our community; we may have a wife who is loving and devoted; and yet we may be the prey to irrational fears or a shuttlecock between opposing and seemingly irreconcilable impulses.

A middle-aged woman sits in the chair next to my desk. Her face is finely chiseled, and she has lines of tension about her mouth. She has been to many doctors and has had many examinations. It is hard to find out just what she complains of. She is underweight. She drives herself hard, sits on many committees, has a strong sense of *noblesse oblige* and a feeling of owing a debt to society for the privileges that she has enjoyed. She often awakens in the middle of the night with a feeling of half pain and half fear, which she locates in the upper mid-abdomen. She thinks that this must be the beginning of the menopause. She has, moreover, been given many injections of estrogens, and they always make her feel better—for a while. A recent gynecological consultant told her that he could find no evidence of the menopause. That has disquieted her. What can it be? She hopes that she is not going to have a nervous breakdown. She does not want to go to a sanitarium. She had a brother who committed suicide. She is really frightened. Only one doctor, a country practitioner, helped her. He did not do much for her, but whatever he did was good. Each new specialist holds out new hope and occasions new disappointment. Here is an opportunity for preventive psychiatry. Who is to provide it? There are about four thousand psychiatrists in the country; about one thousand of them are trained in psychotherapy, and there are millions of such patients.

I am sure that she is familiar to you. She can be of any age or any sex and from any social group—rich, middling, or poor. Is medicine organized to take care of these patients? Everyone now seems ready to admit that they form the largest percentage of all those who consult doctors—from 50 to 75 per cent—the people "without anything the matter with them," who suffer from headache, fatigue, constipation, backache, and all the tiresome list of minor symptoms. Mixed with them, too, are the sufferers from anxiety, from depression, from body overconcern, from hypochondriasis, from various organ neuroses and hysterical conversion symptoms, from obsessions and compulsions, from phobias. They are no crazier than you or I.

What do we do about them? The first thing that we do is to fall right into the trap that these patients set for us. Their one fear is that there is something serious the matter with them. This fear is rivaled by a second, almost as intense, and that is that there is nothing serious the matter with them and that they will be told it is all "just nerves." Now the doctor, being conscientious and well trained, is, of course, zealous not to overlook "anything organic." In his eager search he winds up the patient's anxiety and overconcern. When all the tests come back negative, the doctor, like the patient, gets more and more troubled, because when confronted with symptoms which are "just neurotic" he does not know what to do. He has the impression that when he is faced with what he calls "organic pathology" he knows just what to do, but when he is faced with psychopathology he gets scared and wants to take to the woods or, at least, send for a psychiatrist. In this he reminds me of one of my classmates at medical school who was asked, in an examination in obstetrics, what to do in case of uterine hemorrhage. His answer was brief and to the point. He said: "I'd send for a doctor."

Now why is it that the average M.D. feels so comfortable in the presence of what he calls a frank pneumonia, an acute appendicitis, or even chronic cardiovascular renal disease and so ill at ease when faced by the much more common but perhaps less dramatic neurotic symptoms of his patients? Why, in the first case, does he move swiftly and expertly to the appropriate therapy, while in the second he flounders, delays, and resorts to a variety of ill-considered sedatives, and placebos, such as might be prescribed by any detail man from a drug house? In place of little pink pills, he now trots out an array of hormones, vitamins, and barbiturates which do about as much and as little good as the pink pills and reinforce the patient's fixation on his symptoms.

I suppose the answer to this question is that in the first case the doctor's education has been adequate and in the second case it has not. Added to this is the fact that in the so-called "organic" diseases our knowledge is more precise and our therapy more apparently rational.

What about education in psychiatry? Of the forty-six departments of psychiatry in our medical schools about twenty are at all adequate. Only twenty-four schools have as much as one or more full-time instructors in this department. We now turn out fifty to seventy-five qualified psychiatrists a year, hardly enough to make up the loss from death and retirement. From this number we have to man our state and voluntary hospitals, provide communities with experts in diagnosis and treatment, and train teachers and intellectual leaders. I need hardly tell you that we are falling down on the job. The minimum requirement for institutional work alone is six thousand to seven thousand men. And we could easily absorb twenty thousand to thirty thousand analytically trained psychiatrists, in addition to the paltry four hundred or five hundred we have today. Fortunately, this deficit is about to begin to diminish.

Why is there such a shortage? It is partly related to an over-all shortage of physicians. There is at present a deficit of some one hundred thousand. In the first forty years of this century the population nearly doubled, but the number of licensed physicians increased from one hundred and thirty-two thousand to one hundred and sixty-five thousand only. In other words, the physician-patient ratio has dropped greatly.

The insufficient number of psychiatrists, however, is not wholly a reflection of the lack of physicians. It is in part the result of our teaching methods. In a recent alumni appraisal of psychiatric education replies are given to a questionnaire submitted to four hundred and twelve students who graduated mostly in 1940 from sixty-nine of the seventy-eight approved medical schools of North America.

Here are some characteristic ones:

"Psychiatry is only applied common sense. Why do they teach it in such fancy verbiage?"

"In our school, psychiatry was too easy to pass. It was a cinch course. It was quietly ridiculed by the highly influential professors of surgery and medicine. Suggestible students were thus influenced to adopt the same attitude."

"Clinical contacts with patients were far more meager in psychiatry than in any other specialty."

"Psychiatry cannot be taught from books but only from handling patients. Yet patient-contacts are fewer here than in clinical subjects that you can learn from books."

"Professors of psychiatry talk too much, do too little."

"So many of our instructors were queer ducks that we got to think you had to be queer to go into the specialty."

"There was a general feeling that psychiatrists were all screwy."

And one poor lad's lament was this: "We had numerous instructors," he said, "and they used varying terminology and had varying ideas. What was 'tension' to one teacher was 'anxiety' to another. For that matter, what was gospel to one, was anathema to another. I respect academic freedom, but it is all very confusing."

Of all the grievances, however, the chief one was that the students did not see enough psychoneurotic and minor nonpsychotic cases. I agree with this last complaint. To meet it, in my own teaching, I avoid selecting patients who exhibit so-called classical evidences of psychopathology. They need present no memory defects, no paranoid projections, ideas of reference, retrospective falsifications, *déjà vu* phenomena, delusions, or hallucinations. They merely need to be human beings in trouble.

This is not to say that descriptive psychopathology is unimportant. It is largely the basis of our present nosology, unsatisfactory though it is. But it is the part of psychiatry that is best taught and also, I think, least important for the practicing physician or surgeon. I concur with Whitehorn when he says of psychiatry that it is "at present in a stage of transition" becoming "increasingly a science of psychodynamics, of the understanding of human motivation and the better utilization of human assets and resources, rather than being so exclusively preoccupied as heretofore with psychopathological phenomena."

Accordingly, when a student reports on a patient with rheumatic heart disease and knows all about the T wave and the P-R interval, the sedimentation rate and the presence or absence of rheumatic nodules, I usually ask him what floor does the patient live on, does he go to work by subway and, if the patient is a housewife, how many rooms are there in her apartment, and, if she makes the beds, does she also turn the mattresses. As these questions undoubtedly sound a little queer to most medical students, they probably are explained by the fact that I am listed in the college catalogue as belonging to the department of psychiatry.

It is very hard for the still somewhat callow medical student to get a stereoscopic view of a sick man. Like so many of his teachers he must see a symptom as either "psychogenic" or "organic," as if these were opposite and antithetical concepts. One of his favorite pronouncements is: "There is nothing psychosomatic about this case. The patient had a happy childhood, and the family history is uneventful." At this point I usually interrupt and say: "No childhood is altogether happy, and no family history is uneventful."

Most patients who consult psychiatrists are either very much afraid of something or angry about something, or they want something they cannot have, or they want to have their cake and eat it too—that is, they want irreconcilables. The symptoms they complain of are, therefore, often physiological discharges which serve to relieve tension. Curing the symptom will frequently only increase the tension and necessitate a discharge along another pathway. It is, therefore, necessary to understand what the emotion is that the symptom is trying to relieve and express.

Here is a detailed report of a conversation between a medical student and an instructor. The scene is the sun porch at the end of a male medical ward in one of our large voluntary teaching hospitals. There are about fifteen or twenty fourth-year medical students sitting, or rather lounging, in comfortable armchairs in a semicircular formation. The instructor is seated in a similar chair opposite them. He asks a student to tell the group about the patient whom the student has just spent an hour interviewing and whose clinical record he has studied and now has before him. The student keeps his eye pretty constantly glued on the record for fear of forgetting any important facts.

According to stylized convention he begins: "The patient is an unmarried white male of forty-nine." The instructor interrupts him: "Is the patient a man or a marsupial? Are you a white male, or a medical student?" He allows that he is a medical student and that the patient is a professor of Romance languages. The student goes on: "He came to the hospital for a bleeding duodenal ulcer. X-rays show deformity of the cap." But the instructor stops him again and says: "What university does the professor belong to?" The student then mentions one of the oldest and best known of the eastern universities. At this point the instructor inquires why a professor of one of our most famous universities is a patient on the public ward. Why not in a private or semiprivate room? The student does not know the answer but says that the patient was admitted through the accident ward, where he came for a minor injury. He hastens to add that that was merely coincidental; when they discovered in the accident ward that he had typical signs and symptoms of a duodenal ulcer, they sent him into the hospital for investigation. The student, like a hound picking up the scent, is off again on the subject of the deformity of the duodenal cap. The instructor, however, relentlessly pursues his Socratic way.

He inquires rather flatly: "Why was he brought to the accident ward?"

The student replies: "For a cut on his hand, but that had nothing to do with his admission to the hospital. He was *admitted* because of his bleeding ulcer."

INSTRUCTOR: "How did he cut his hand?"

STUDENT: "He fell out of bed."

INSTRUCTOR: "Why does a forty-nine-year-old professor of Romance languages fall out of bed—especially if unmarried?"

STUDENT: "He's very fat."

INSTRUCTOR: "Do you mean he was too big for his bed and rolled out?"

STUDENT: "Yes, that's it."

INSTRUCTOR: "How can you cut your hand by falling out of bed?"

STUDENT: "He fell on a milk bottle."

INSTRUCTOR: "What was he doing with a milk bottle under his bed?"

STUDENT: "I don't know."

The instructor continues: "Why is he so fat?"

STUDENT: "From drinking cough syrup. He gained about sixty pounds in a year. He takes the cough syrup, which contains codeine, because of epigastric pain caused by his ulcer, and it's the ulcer that is responsible for his being in the hospital."

The patient is now brought in, in a wheel chair. He is a mountain of a man with an intellectual brow and large limpid eyes. He has a small button of a mouth. The instructor shakes hands with him. His hands are moist and tremulous. He is a glib and voluble talker, full of rationalizations. Although the instructor does his best to put him at his ease, he is obviously on the defensive and is much ashamed of his codeine addiction. He explains that he has taken the cough medicine because of his intractable and excruciating pain, which comes on mostly at night. His illness and, of course, his addiction, have cost him his job, and he is now without a position on the faculty. This has confronted him with new and very real problems of livelihood.

When the patient has been wheeled out of the room, the instructor discusses with his class the emotional aspects of the professor's illness, more specifically, what careful physiological and psychiatric research have revealed about the relationship of dependent needs to ulcer formation.

I have told this story not, of course, to hold a poor medical student up to ridicule; nothing is more unforgivable in a teacher. My object is to bring out a familiar and prevailing attitude in medicine—often more pronounced in the older members of the staff than in the younger group of residents and interns: the "either-or" attitude, the "psychogenic" versus "organic." It is a pedantic, traditional, academic attitude that has little to do with the facts presented us by nature. The case which I have just outlined is one in point—an example of a gross structural lesion, intrinsically bound up with a man's personality and with the way he leads his life.

If psychiatry is to permeate medicine and surgery and the specialties, as I believe it should, then it must be taught not in one department of a medical school but in all departments. It is not enough to expose medical students to a few catatonic schizophrenics or patients suffering from involutional melancholia and expect them to emerge with an understanding of the complexities of human personality and of the motive power behind human behavior. And yet, such understanding is necessary for everyone engaged in the healing arts as well as in the science of medicine.

The experience and acumen of the old-time practitioner is a good thing—now rather rare—but it is not enough. There is new knowledge that can be taught and there are new technics that can be applied in practice. Symptoms such as vomiting, constipation, diarrhea, sweating, breathlessness, palpitation, loss of appetite, constant hunger, obesity, etc., should always be thought of as expressing some emotional need, as well as betraying some diseased organ or organ system.

The fact that treatment is time-consuming and that results are often meager is no reason for withholding this knowledge from students. It takes a long time to arrest tuberculosis, except in its very early stages; a long time to control diabetes; and we have not yet learned to replace a small contracted kidney with a new one through which the blood flows freely. And yet no one will doubt that the more the physician knows about the mechanisms involved in these illnesses, the more he will be able to do for his patients. Stacked side by side, the results achieved by psychotherapy would probably measure pretty well against many other forms of medical treatment.

I have dealt, so far, with teaching medical students and not with teaching men already in practice. We, in this country, have never really tackled the problem of postgraduate medical education seriously enough. Once a man is established in practice, it is ordinarily difficult for him to do more than attend a few condensed refresher courses. But there is a great need for expanding this sort of service to the profession, and psychiatric training should have a prominent place in such programs.

There is another side to the problem if we are to bring good preventive medicine, including psychiatry, to more people earlier. Not only in medical schools but throughout hospitals phychiatry must be at home, instead of remaining isolated, esoteric, and outlandish. Are our hospitals too frozen in their brick and mortar and in the brick and mortar of their administrative habits to adapt themselves to the changing needs of society? I should like to venture the opinion that the position of the hospital in relation to the community must be studied with a fresh and open and socially oriented mind, if it is to approximate the requirements of the present and the future.

Just as we have divided our teaching into what is considered psychiatric and what is not, so have we divided our hospitals and outpatient departments. It is my conviction, shared by many of my colleagues, that no general hospital should longer be without its psychiatric department and that the cross-fertilization of medicine and psychiatry should go on by constant contact between the two types of physicians—on the wards, in consultations, in the lunchroom, and in the doctors' smoking-room. The end in view should be one kind of physician. Whether he customarily uses a scalpel or a stethoscope, he can also be trained in certain indispensable principles of psychiatry.

The outpatient department is one of the places where preventive psychiatry may best be practiced. As long as it remains the stepchild of the institution, shoved into a basement or wing to which its hereditary origin seems to have consigned it, it will fail in this function; for the modern outpatient department is the offspring of the eighteenth-century dispensary, an institution separate from the hospital and often in competition with it. It should actually be in the very center of the building, where it belongs. As it has been physically isolated, so has it been spiritually and intellectually. It is seldom manned by the best talent—often by young men ambitious for promotion or by older, dull gentlemen who have never been admitted to the inner sanctum of the house staff. True, the professor and the attending physicians sometimes do penance by putting in a few hours in the outpatient department, but they do so more to show the young men that they too are interested than because they really are. The main work of these more mature and gifted physicians is not centered in the outpatient department.

I need not labor this point further. It can be summed up by saying that until the outpatient is directed by a full-time man of highest quality, whose heart and soul are in his work, and who hand-picks his associates, only second-rate clinical and investigative work can be expected. The first plan for the future, therefore, must encompass such a change in staff.

Part of this change will also involve a closer co-operation with the inpatient department, which can be accomplished only by a continuity of staffs. At present the best continuity is supplied by the unit record system, a rather recent innovation in outpatient departments. Until a few years ago it was customary to have an inpatient record meticulously kept by interns and residents and an outpatient card on which inadequate notes were entered. But continuity of records is not enough unless there is also continuity of staffs.

Turning now to a second relic of the past: sweet charity. Its musty fetid breath fills every corner of the average outpatient department. It has done more to poison the atmosphere than anything else. It is an indignity to patients and staff alike. The patients sit on hard benches and waste hours, as if their time were worth nothing. The doctors who work for nothing would rather be in their offices earning money or in their laboratories earning fame or just playing golf. Even the most humane of them develop the tendency to push patients around, to pass the buck, so to speak, by many "referrals" and many consultations. There is a constant shift of responsibility. In this connection my friend, Dr. Henry B. Richardson, made the salty observation that when a clinic record reaches a certain thickness, a certain net weight, the patient is usually referred to a psychiatrist.

The hospitals, to make ends meet, to carry the load of the outpatient department, have had to develop a deficit economy and soon learned to soak the rich in order to pay for the poor—a system which works to the disadvantage of both.

The more modern pay clinic, even if run at a loss, and the few self-supporting diagnostic clinics that exist are efforts to meet this unhealthy situation.

The fact that outpatient departments are products of large cities has, of course, had its effect on their character. It has led to overcrowding and to case loads far in excess of capacities of the professional staffs. The natural consequence of this has been long waiting on the part of patients and hurried, slipshod work on the part of doctors. A recent effort to correct this evil is the introduction of the appointment system, which, I am sure you will agree with me, is essential to running an efficient clinic.

Each one of the evils of the past has, in some measure, been met by reforms, introduced into our better outpatient departments. These reforms provide us with a pattern for the ideal outpatient department of the future. The characteristics of such a department should be:

A centrally located clinic, manned by skilled workers of top grade who are adequately paid for their services.

A clinic run, not on a deficit basis, but one supported by insurance, a community fund, or taxation.

A clinic run on an appointment basis, divided into units capable of handling a specified case load.

Each unit would be staffed by a certain number of internists, psychiatrists, and other specialists. Again the infiltrating process would take place. The psychopaths, the feeble-minded, the dilapidated, and the deteriorated who exist in every community but who slow up the work of effective and preventive psychotherapy would be handled in other clinics.

We have data available for the approximate costs of such units. I will not now take the time to go into the detailed plans, but I should mention that each unit is scaled to handle from seventy-five hundred to eight thousand patients per year at an approximate cost of $20 per patient. Assuming that 20 per cent of a community needs the attention of a doctor, then one such unit could serve a population of forty thousand. It would be coordinated with an inpatient service of one hundred and fifty beds in which psychiatric as well as medical and surgical ones are included. Such a reorganization of our hospital practices would do much to bring early and preventive psychiatric care to the community.

Up to this point I have discussed certain needed changes in the organization of our teaching and hospital services, if we are to bring psychotherapy to more people earlier. The essence of what I have said is that in all departments of medical schools and hospitals there must be an infiltration of psychiatric thought, so that it no longer remains an esoteric, outlandish jargon unrelated to the workaday lives of our patients. But even if these changes were accomplished, they would not be enough. The more our knowledge of emotional maladjustment grows, the more widespread we find it to be. It is probable that the greater the number of doctors equipped to diagnose and treat such disturbances, the greater the number of patients who will demand and require such help. In this it is like dentistry. Dental caries in our civilization is universal. If dental treatment and prophylaxis took as long as psychiatric care, we would be put to it to find enough dentists, even though there are seventy-two thousand of them now in practice, as compared with four thousand psychiatrists.

The result of the shortage of psychiatrists and the apparently inexhaustible supply of patients has been to drive psychiatric fees up. That is an inevitable consequence in any competitive enterprise. It has also created the false impression that neurotic illness is more prevalent among the well-to-do who can afford treatment and the idle who have time for it than it is among the working and white-collar classes. There is no evidence to support this belief or the other conventionally held one that psychoneuroses are of more frequent occurrence in women than in men.

Another consequence of the undersupply of physicians trained in psychotherapy and of the great demand for their services is that nonmedical lay groups have begun more and more to enter the field.

I am not now talking of the lunatic fringe of mystics, occultists, health faddists, crystal gazers, and radio doctors who people the land and gnaw at the bones of our failures. I am referring to a more responsible and legitimate group, many of them better equipped to practice psychotherapy than the average physician untrained in this work. They are the clinical psychologists and also the psychiatric social workers. Since both are brought in constant contact with emotionally disturbed persons, it is natural and inevitable that they will sooner or later be drawn into a therapeutic relationship. Their services are greatly needed. I myself am not shocked at the idea of lay therapists. Many of them, from native sensitiveness, intelligence, interest, and experience are well qualified for this work. But it is better if they collaborate with a licensed physician in the treatment of their cases.

Anyone who has worked in a psychiatric outpatient department or in a rehabilitation clinic appreciates how invaluable are the uses of a well-trained psychiatric social worker. They are often the mainstay of these departments. Without their help we would be put to it not only to get accurate data about patients but also to explore the possibilities of occupational and recreational facilities.

As for the clinical psychologist, no up-to-date psychiatrist would want to get along without his help. He has become to the psychiatrist what the roentgenologist is to the internist. Or, using another analogy, the position of the clinical psychologist in a psychiatric department is like that of a surgical pathologist in a department of surgery or a biochemist or physiologist in a department of medicine or gynecology. But not only should he be used to help solve practical problems of diagnosis and to explore the resources of personality, he should first and foremost be encouraged to pursue his own researches. Too many gifted psychologists are now being forced into the position of therapists, where through lack of medical training they often remain frustrated, instead of using their energies and skills to push back the walls of our ignorance with methods of relative precision.

Some of our present cherished nosological conceptions may have to be revised as the result of the studies and observations of clinical psychologists. I have in mind, especially, that large group of patients on whom various projective tests reveal an otherwise undisclosed latent schizophrenia.

The ideal therapeutic team consists of a psychiatrist, a clinical psychologist, and a psychiatric social worker. Their interest and emphasis complement one another. I believe that before long the enlightened internist as well will avail himself of these increasingly useful ancillary disciplines.

I have spoken a good deal about therapy, but I do not wish to overstress it at the cost of exploring the possibilities of prevention. To all physicians, whatever their specialty, that must always remain their first challenge and their first concern.

As part of the centennial celebration of the New York Academy of Medicine each one of its important committees held a series of seminars, or institutes, extending over several days. One of these, sponsored by the Committee on Public Health Relations, dealt with the "Realities in Preventive Psychiatry." No one lost sight of the fact that Dr. E. H. L. Corwin, who chose this provocative title, was playing the psychiatrists at their own game and demanding that they face the realities of their own profession.

To prevent a disease, two things are required: knowledge and organization. As for the first, we need to know the cause of the disease and its means of transmission, and we should have information about the number of susceptibles in the community. Armed with such facts, we begin a preventive campaign, if we have the organization to apply them. Let us, for a moment, look at mental and emotional disturbances as though they were pandemic, which I believe in truth they are. Can we put our finger on the cause of them? No, not in any simple way. But can we say that the tubercle bacillus alone causes tuberculosis or that the pneumococcus causes pneumonia? If that were true, all of us would be sufferers from these maladies.

Even if we do not know their exact cause, what we can do is to describe the setting out of which these mental and emotional disorders arise. About that we have a good deal of information. We know that the seeds of later psychoneurotic illness are sown in early childhood, that lack of tender maternal care is the surest preparation for later trouble. We know that these disturbances are passed on from parent to offspring, not through the genes primarily, but through the transmission of anxiety and through imitation and unconscious identification. We know that the susceptibility to them is as universal as it is for measles, that all human beings are prone to develop, at some time or other, neurotic disturbances, either in the form of organized psychoneuroses or in the form that we now call psychosomatic. We know that susceptibility varies at different periods in life and in response to different kinds of traumata. The most susceptible period is infancy and early childhood. It is also the one in which prophylactic measures are most productive of good. Adolescence with its storm and stress is another period of high susceptibility or low resistance. The chemical and physiological changes characteristic of this age give rise to new sensations, new tensions, and new drives that seek correspondingly new outlets and satisfactions. And yet they come at a time when adult modes of expression are in the main denied by society. The adolescent is, therefore, a restless animal, in a state of revolt. It is no coincidence that delinquent behavior is so common in him. Often for the first time he takes measure of his parents and finds them far from perfect or infallible. He struggles to free himself from his own infantile dependence. His hostilities crowd to the front as never before. He may be concerned in a brooding, almost obsessional way, with the eternal verities, with thoughts on death and immortality, accompanied by a strong upsurge of religious emotion and idealism or an aversion to past religious teachings and practices. In this state of turmoil and confusion and unrealistic thinking, not unlike that of a schizophrenic, the adolescent tests himself out on the cold world around him. What he sees is disappointing, disillusioning. He finds intense competition, cruel injustice, and special privilege. The more chaotic the world, the greater his own bewilderment. No wonder that he tries to shape it to fit his fantasies and that he often comes to grief.

Again the period of involution, the climacterium in both sexes, is one of extreme vulnerability to emotional disturbance. Many of our patients react to the chemical and physiological changes of this time of life with states of tension, irritability, depression, and a variety of other manifestations. In some, they merge imperceptibly into the disabilities of presenility and senility with characteristic loss of memory, body overconcern, tendency to paranoid delusions, and a general shrinking of intellectual and emotional horizons.

This is not to say, of course, that susceptibility exists only at these times. It is always with us, though usually more pronounced during the cataclysmic epochs. As susceptibility varies, so does the intensity of the stimulus required to call forth disturbance. For an infant in arms, a mother's absence from home may suffice; for a five-year-old, the birth of a brother or sister, a parent's death, or the departure of a beloved nurse may pull the trigger; for a preadolescent, the absence of his father at war or the father's drunkenness or the divorce of his parents. Later in life, an unsuccessful sexual encounter, an unhappy love affair, a change in routine (as, for example, after induction into the army), physical illness, loss of home or partner or money—any one of these may be as traumatic as the explosion of a land mine or many hazardous missions through enemy flak. But these experiences are not the causes of the neuroses. They are the releasing mechanism of previously prepared reactions.

If we are to prevent such reactions, our familiarity with them and our understanding of them, even if far more adequate than it now is, would not suffice. We cannot withstand the onslaught of an invading army by tactics and logistics alone. We need a manœuvrable force as well. In the war against these illnesses we have no such force. We have no shock troops and few reserves. In the very front line of defense should stand the practicing physician, and he must be trained and disciplined not to turn tail in rout at the first sign of the enemy.

The front battalions that I should deploy are the obstetricians and the prenatal-care clinics. Here is an opportunity for a mighty resistance. Every woman who is going to have a baby should be prepared for the event by relieving her of anxiety. She should be fully instructed before delivery on the rudiments of infant care, especially on how to hold and carry a baby. She should practice first on decoys, then on live models. She should be reassured about her fears of labor. And her husband should be interviewed and shown a few newborn babies, the redder and the more wrinkled the better.

Behind the obstetricians there should be waves of pediatricians, trained in psychiatry. There is only a small band of them now. But what they have done is invaluable. There are several pediatricians of my acquaintance who practically never have a feeding problem in their practices because they know how to treat mothers. These men are able to allay maternal worries over thumb-sucking, masturbation, constipation, tantrums, and nightmares, and, by so doing, they help to stop them. One human and humane pediatrician in a large New York hospital is in the habit of writing "T.L.C." on certain charts. These initials stand for "tender, loving care," which he prescribes at regular intervals and in definite doses, as he might have ordered paregoric. He is convinced that he has shortened illness and reduced mortality by this prescription. I am told that this is now a common procedure in more advanced institutions.

It can no longer be doubted that mothering is essential

to an infant's proper development. When babies are separated from their mothers and are placed in the sterilized, impersonal atmosphere of foundling homes, almost without exception they develop subsequent psychiatric disturbances and become asocial, delinquent, feeble-minded, or psychotic. When hospitalization occurs during the first year of life, the resulting impairment seems irremediable. The better equipped and the more hygienic the institution, the worse it appears to be for the child. The reason we have not known this fact long ago is that in the foundling homes of former days sanitary conditions were so bad and infant mortality so high that many of the children did not grow up to become defectives. Even the most destitute family offers more mental and emotional stimulation than the usual impersonal hospital ward.

But to go on with my plan of battle. Supporting the pediatricians and ready to replace them, when they are expended, are the divisions of internists, surgeons, and specialists, each equipped with suitable weapons to counterattack and to meet the enemy where he actually is, not where they want him to be. They will be prepared to carry the war into enemy territory. The real field of prevention is in the home, in marriage, in schools, in colleges, in the law courts, in the factory, as well as in hospitals. Here we will need powerful allies. In this war everyone is involved. It is no longer a war of professional soldiers alone. Just as in the prevention of tuberculosis or typhoid or smallpox, the co-operation of the public is essential, so here, too, the education and morale of the layman is almost a prerequisite of our effectiveness in the battle against psychiatric disorders.

CHAPTER XII

Medical Information and Misinformation

THE days of such sentiments as "The public be damned" or "The people want to be humbugged" have gone with the bowler, the bustle, and the Bowery. It is now generally agreed that a democracy depends upon an enlightened electorate.

This conviction has penetrated all walks of life. Conscientious medical men take their responsibility in this regard seriously. They have, moreover, unmasked themselves. They have shaved off their beards, taken off their clericals, and stand before the public for what they are—ready even to expose their own ignorance. This is all to the good.

There is, moreover, an elaborate organization by which the man on the street can inform himself of medical and scientific discoveries and developments. The press has increasingly adopted a policy of accuracy and professionalism. Such writers as Albert Deutsch, Waldemar Kaempffert, and William Laurence are doing a fine service in presenting and interpreting scientific facts and theories to the untrained reader.

The American Medical Association and the various state and county societies, through committees on public relations, carry on active campaigns to enlighten the people in matters of health. The magazine *Hygeia* is one of many mediums through which the American Medical Association aims to educate laymen.

In New York the Academy of Medicine has for years taken a leading part in furthering the welfare of our citizens by acquainting them with advances in medical knowledge. Its Bureau of Public Information sponsors annual lectures to the laity, delivered by recognized authorities. For more than ten years these lectures have been published in book form.

Under the able and imaginative leadership of the late Dr. James Alexander Miller and of Dr. E. H. L. Corwin, the academy's Committee on Public Health Relations has for thirty-eight years studiously and energetically addressed itself to various health problems, covering the whole range of medical interest, as Dr. Corwin puts it, from nutrition to sewage disposal. This committee has co-operated with many social agencies and has often influenced important legislation.

The faculty of the Harvard Medical School has, for many years, offered an annual lecture series. Wherever adult education is fostered—for example, at Cooper Union or at the New School for Social Research—part of the curriculum is likely to be devoted to medical topics.

One can hardly turn on the radio without hearing some doctor—sandwiched, to be sure, between a honeyed crooner and a splash of hot jazz—delivering a talk on such subjects as rheumatic heart disease, the feeding problems of infants, or the sulpha drugs.

The movies have taken up the vogue of medical enlightenment and through documentary shorts show us the life-cycle of the malarial plasmodium or a fascinating picture of the discovery and preparation of penicillin.

Drug houses publish expensive illustrated brochures on the dismal effects of avitaminosis on the white rat or on the phenomenal changes in the capon induced by testosterone.

Health centers, maternity centers, municipal and state

departments of health, and the United States Public Health Service all contribute their share in the dissemination of knowledge.

In addition, there are various special societies, such as the National Tuberculosis Association, the American Heart Association, the American Cancer Society, the National Association To Control Epilepsy, and the National Committee for Mental Hygiene. Each one of these societies—through meetings, lectures, books, pamphlets, press releases, and all the modern technics of publicity—strives to carry home to the public the truth and significance of its high purpose.

The list that I have just furnished is admittedly an impressive one, though it is certainly far from complete. The public is fortunate to have at its service so many sources of factual information. Anyone who is literate and in the possession of his faculties can inform himself on many medical matters. He who runs may read. In the face of this avalanche of information, it is indeed hard to see how the man on the street withstands enlightenment.

And yet he often does. Why is this so? Why, in spite of all of these efforts, is there still so much medical misinformation?

Let us take a look at this problem. I have already enumerated the many channels of accurate medical information. Each one, however—whether printed, spoken, or photographic—may also be a source of misinformation. Although newspapers have greatly improved their handling of medical news, a defect that still remains lies in the reporting of half-truths taken out of context and then blown up for sensational-headline purposes. For example, a young reporter will attend a medical meeting at which papers are presented on the treatment of general paresis or tabes with penicillin. He has probably been given a handout and, therefore, the body of the text will quote

Dr. X and Dr. Y quite correctly, stressing all of their tentative and cautious conclusions—and yet whoever writes the headlines may head the column with "Doctors Find New Cure for Syphilis."

On the written words of my medical colleagues I have, naturally, few comments to make—except to say that I often cannot understand them myself. When I cannot, I like to think that it results from the manner of presentation rather than from my own stupidity. After a fair number of trials, including the reading of several popular pieces, I have only just discovered a scientific paper on the Rh factor that has made this complicated subject more or less clear to me. Now the Rh factor should be a matter of great concern to the public. But how they can be made to understand it unless scientists learn to write plain English for public consumption, I cannot imagine.

The writing of good English is a difficult art and like all other arts requires a lifetime of devotion. Sir Osbert Sitwell says that an author can never take a vacation. He describes how he wrestles with his creative angel in the small hours of the morning and quotes H. G. Wells, who once remarked to him: "If you are in difficulties with a book, try the element of surprise . . . attack it at an hour when it isn't expecting it." Such dedication to the art of expression is hardly possible for the already preoccupied physician, teacher, or research worker.

But there are other reasons that militate against the medical fraternity's learning to write clearly and easily for the public. Until rather recently such activity was more or less frowned upon in this country. We are a nation of professionals and specialists. If you are a doctor, people do not generally accept you as a writer, and vice versa. It makes them uncomfortable to have to think in more than one category at a time. Perhaps you have heard of the professor's advice to the student who decided to practice dermatology. He said: "You must be so identified with your specialty that when people hear your name, they will begin to itch."

Our English cousins have not been so single-minded. It is nothing for a wholesale greengrocer to be also the greatest amateur expert on butterflies. British scientists have long taken their responsibility to the public seriously, just as our nuclear physicists have begun to do. The Huxleys and Jeanses and Eddingtons and Haldanes have not lost stature through their popular writings. It has been an admirable custom in England for the greatest scientists to give lectures to children during the Christmas holidays.

In medical circles such names as Rollston, Lord Horder, Lord Moynihan, Michael Foster, Lauder-Brunton, and others have been an adornment to medical literature, as Osler's and Cushing's have been here.

There is a stiffness and a scholasticism and a love of cant in the professional writing of medical men that interferes with their getting their thoughts over to the public. When they do relax a bit and come down from the lecture platform and talk simply—even committing that final outrage of using the first person singular—then they run smack into the raised-eyebrow department of their colleagues. But, tell me, how are you going to catch the interest, say, of several million American women who should be taught something about the problems of adolescence, if you address them in the dry, impersonal tones of a schoolteacher? One has to approximate their own idiom and do it without cheapness and with strict adherence to fact. Admittedly that is an art.

The art, of course, is well known to many professional writers. More and more of them are writing on more and more medical topics for more and more magazines—weeklies, monthlies, pulps, and slicks. Sometimes they do it amazingly well. Sometimes it is a source of embarrassment to us medical people and of disservice to the public. A few years ago one of our popular weeklies published a piece on hypnosis—referring to it as the shining new weapon of psychiatry and mentioning the name of the director of a New York hospital in which hypnosis was practiced. The poor man was deluged with pleas for help, and patients came to the hospital doors from as far as Alaska.

These lay writers on medical subjects are quick to pick up anything of news value. They will often call on us and consult us with great earnestness about some subject of timely interest. Some of them come prepared and have at least a background of reading and library research. Others try to draw us out in interviews. "Doctor, what do you think about high blood pressure?" "Why are American women nervous?" "What is wrong with our children, anyway?" "What about insomnia? Is it on the increase?"

No doubt, each one of these topics would make excellent copy—but the medical man is naturally wary of such interviews. With a little experience he will soon learn to discriminate between the serious writer and the hack. He will also be chary of the re-write man who has a love for jazzing up the stuff we give him. One of them recently asked me whether it was not true that the rich were more frequently neurotic than the poor. My answer was a dry one. I said we had no adequate statistics but that it was my impression that there was no correlation between neurotic illness and income. The interview came back: "Neurotic illness is not an occupational disease of the idle rich who get their only calluses from cutting coupons." This kind of phony writing we do not like, and, moreover, it is not necessary in order to interest and instruct the lay reader.

One might hope that collaborators could be found to work together. But Gilberts and Sullivans are rare in this world. It is more likely that we will have to learn to set our own words to music. At least there is an increasing tendency among responsible and authoritative medical men to address the public directly, because they look upon it as part of their job to do so.

To turn now for a moment to the radio, this ubiquitous instrument has become a valuable means of transmitting medical knowledge. Doctors are, of course, loath to accept the sponsorship of commercial houses which may use them to advertise their wares. We do not want to become the champions of a particular brand of whiskey or tooth paste. But such a program as "The Doctors Talk It Over," sponsored by the Lederle Laboratories, is something else. These programs are broadcast to the medical profession by its leaders. No doubt many laymen as well listen to them with profit. They cover important and timely topics, and the list of speakers is a distinguished one.

But, again, the art of broadcasting is not native to medicos. Even when they conquer their mike fright, they are often dull, prosy, and prolix. Here is a sample from a radio talk a doctor gave one weekday afternoon to housewives:

> "Although I stressed organic disease, one must not lose sight of the early symptoms of behavior disorders, which are amenable to proper management under the guidance of your physician. But in addition to behavior problems *per se*, changes in behavior may themselves indicate organic disease."
>
> Do you understand what he means? Do you think the housewives understood? Do you think they will be able to tell a "behavior problem *per se*" when they see one?

This quotation, and the comment on it, are taken from that lucid and luminous book, *The Art of Plain Talk*, by Rudolf Flesch.

But if the amateur on the radio has his limitations in this field, so has the professional. I listened to a medical radio drama not long since: An ambitious and extravagant wife, egged on by her children, was urging her poor, tired husband to greater and greater efforts in order to keep up with the Joneses. Finally the camel's back broke. The husband had a heart attack, accompanied by the usual stertorous radio music.

Enter Dr. Pill, who reads the riot act to the assembled and terrified family and makes the poor victim feel that his life is worth about thirty cents. He finally departs, leaving behind him an admonishing atmosphere of guilt and gloom. "Rotten medicine," I said to myself. It seems to be about as hard for a radio actor to talk like a doctor as for a doctor to talk like a radio actor. Perhaps technics can be worked out to stage medical dramas on the air with a more genuine ring to them.

Of the screen, I will have little to say. I have already mentioned some of the excellent documentary shorts. The full-length cinema productions of medical subjects seldom quite come off—from our point of view. Crowded houses and box-office receipts need have no relation to scientific truth—except perhaps an inverse one. When Hollywood learns that great art is never the enemy of truth, we will have better movies and better public education.

I cannot leave this part of my discussion without a word on the advertising game. It is a game, and the public is its plaything. We are hammered, beaten, and exhausted into brand consciousness. "Buy Vita Loaf. It's got vitamins! It's chockful of body-building, bone-building, energy-building vitamins!" Or "Use Hormone Skin Cream. If you want love interest to thrive, massage each tiny ripple of your body daily with this scientific wonder cream. Just watch the wrinkles fade out. Glamorize your skin. Be radiant!"

As Professor S. I. Hayakawa puts it: "Advertising has become, in short, the art of overcoming us with words . . .

we are sold daydreams with every bottle of mouth-wash, and delusions of grandeur with every package of breakfast-food."

I need hardly comment on the fact that—in spite of the regulations of the Federal Trade Commission and the Pure Food and Drug Act—these commercial plugs are a prolific source of medical misinformation.

So much for the technics of transmitting medical knowledge. May I now turn to less specific but more far-reaching reasons for misunderstanding on the part of the public?

In a communication system between men, what goes in at one end is not always what comes out at the other. With the use of such symbols as words and pictures, there is always the chance of misunderstanding. These symbols are at best approximations and conventions and will be weighted according to the connotative experience of both transmitter and receiver. I wish I were a student of semantics, so that I could go further into this important aspect of misunderstanding. Perhaps I can illustrate my point best by suggesting that a red banner means one thing to a bull in a bull ring, another to Bilbo and Rankin, and something quite different to Messrs. Molotov and Stalin.

A principal source of misunderstanding and, therefore, of misinformation lies in the misinterpretation of symbols.

Language, according to Hayakawa, performs a double task. It *informs* us and it *affects* our feelings. The informative part of language depends upon our ability to use noises as symbols. But some noises that we make are presymbolic—that is, they express and invoke feelings in ourselves and in others. As Hayakawa says, they are "the equivalent of screams, howls, purrs, and gibbering." It is, of course, a fallacy to think that one word has but one meaning.

The City Council of Cambridge, Massachusetts, "unanimously passed a resolution (in December, 1939) making it illegal 'to possess, harbor, sequester, introduce or transport, within the city limits, any book, map, magazine, newspaper, pamphlet, handbill, or circular containing the word Lenin or Leningrad.' " In other parts of the world farther from the Hub of the Universe, the sound "Lenin" might not be so dangerous to make. Or again, according to Stuart Chase: "State Senator John McNaboe of New York bitterly opposed a bill for the control of syphilis in May, 1937, because he feared that 'the innocence of children might be corrupted by a widespread use of the term. . . . This particular word creates a shudder in every decent woman and decent man.' "

I doubt whether the sound of the word "syphilis" caused a shudder in Schaudinn, who discovered its cause, or in Ehrlich, who discovered its cure. The fact is that most of the sounds we make both denote and connote something.

Medical language has a peculiarly affective quality, because anything connected with our health is likely to arouse strong feelings in us—especially of anxiety. If we have suffered a heart attack or if a woman has discovered a lump in her breast or if our soldier son comes home from the army depressed, dissatisfied, and at odds with himself —then such words as "coronary thrombosis," "tumor," or "psychoneurosis" may arouse great anxiety in us.

Physicians are often unaware how vast this reservoir of anxiety is and how frail the barriers that keep it back. Their lightest word, even their most efficiently objective report of findings, may do more damage than their medicines do good. This ever present anxiety, of course, interferes with understanding and is responsible for a great deal of misinformation. It has led to an overemphasis on physical symptoms and to a demand that treatment be directed primarily at the offending organ—rather than at the whole person. People take what they can take in the way of information, but if facts are too distressing, they ignore them, distort them, or even find it necessary to abuse those who impart them. We want to kill the messenger who brings the bad tidings.

If general medical facts call out strong emotional responses, how much more strongly does anything that has to do with psychiatry! We physicians, and especially those of us who are interested in mental health, will have to keep this constantly in mind in addressing the public. There is a widespread horror of mental and emotional illness, an intense desire to be looked upon as normal, a fear of what others will think or say. In some small communities the dread of being seen going to a psychiatrist would be great enough to keep people away from him—even if there were one to consult.

There is no doubt that this attitude is responsible for confusion, misapprehension, and delay in seeking psychiatric help. I have just had a letter from a woman—unknown to me— in Texas, who writes: "I believe that most of the education of the public must come from the average physician. But they are at present more ignorant of this phase of medicine than a layman who has had even a slight acquaintance with it through some member of his family who has had psychiatric treatment."

Perhaps her allegation is unjust, though it cannot be denied that a trusted and enlightened family physician would be the best instructor in matters of mental health and would be in the most favorable position to allay anxiety, if he were not himself a prey to it. What I have said of the family doctor could also be said of the public health nurse.

The double meaning of words to which I have alluded is, of course, not conferred upon them by the hearer alone. Much of what medical men say and write about is controversial and is overlaid with strong feeling. This is inevitable in a living science. Disagreement exists chiefly in the frontiers of knowledge. Where methods are empirical, where experiment and predictability are not yet possible, where scientific fact is unsupported by adequate theory—there will be differences of opinion and disputation. It will not surprise us, therefore, that in such fields as allergy, for instance, there is a good deal of general misinformation. And especially is this true in psychiatry, where methods are less precise, statistics hard to come by, theoretical conceptions tentative. We disagree among ourselves—and hotly, too—on such matters as psychoanalysis, shock therapy, and others. About them, therefore, we find many fantastic popular misconceptions.

I began this chapter with an enumeration of the many excellent sources of accurate medical information, most of them stemming from organized medicine. The techniques for the dissemination of knowledge were discussed, with particular reference to writing, radio, and the screen. Each one of these can also be a source of misinformation. I made a respectful bow to our best lay writers on scientific subjects and analyzed some of the difficulties that confront the medical man who attempts to address the public directly. I also delivered a well-deserved kick at the commercial plug which, in its effort to brand brand-consciousness upon us, has little interest in truth.

I then went on to a discussion of some of the difficulties inherent in communication between men. I pointed out that many words have two meanings—one meaning informs and the other arouses feelings in the hearer. It is a fallacy to think that a given word has only one meaning. Furthermore, the hearer will understand only what he can take. If his anxiety is aroused—as it often is in matters of health—he will be confused and may defend himself against enlightenment. This fact must constantly be kept in mind by those of us who are concerned with mental hygiene. Disagreement, however, is bound to occur in those branches of science in which facts are less well established and theories less well supported by them. That is what I have tried to convey up to this point.

Now where do we go from here? How can we improve our methods of public education and thus strengthen the hand of medicine?

We can strive for more honest professionalism on the part of lay writers and for the use of straightforward, plain English on the part of medical ones. We should certainly foster and encourage collaboration between these groups. Perhaps it is utopian to think that movie magnates can be persuaded of their great responsibility and opportunity or can be made to realize that the truth is actually more interesting and dramatic than their fictions.

Although the advance of science, so often confused with technology, depends first and foremost on ideas and on genius, organization and equipment are of vital importance, and they take money. Private funds are no longer so lavish as they once were. The whole relation of medical research and education to state and federal money will have to be worked out. Our legislators need to learn that uncertain tenure, civil-service restrictions, inadequate pay, and short-term appropriations are not a congenial soil for the growth of ideas. While the medical profession is rightfully apprehensive about being absorbed by government, its fears have led to politically reactionary and often misleading propaganda. This has been of no service to the profession itself or to the public who look to it trustingly, but perhaps mistakenly, for wise leadership in matters social and economic.

In psychiatry especially, our thinking has been perhaps too much oriented toward the individual patient and not enough toward the community in which he lives. Often his illness is a symptom of a sick society. The prevention of mental illness is the most essential task of the community. It is not one that psychiatrists—even if their number were increased tenfold—can accomplish without the help and understanding of other responsible citizens, especially those in positions of leadership in industry, labor, religion, law, and education—particularly education. The classroom teachers in our public schools could be more influential than any other group if they could be given some real insight and understanding.

In the long history of medicine, we physicians are but characters in the play called *As You Desire Me*. When society believes in evil spirits, we wear masks and beat drums to frighten them away; when it is persuaded of possession by witches, we bore holes in our patients' skulls to let the witches out; when it is given to materialism and worships the dynamo, we become engineers who approach the study of disease with mathematical equations and curves drawn on graph paper; when the emotional problems of living confront us on all sides, we turn to psychosomatic medicine.

Finally, when society is forced by events to recognize its own disorder, then we physicians reluctantly crawl out of our libraries and laboratories and consulting rooms to talk to the people directly. Such a time is now with us. I believe that we have a contribution to make, if we can only master the technics of communication.

We know—from biological evidence alone—that the garnering of the stock piles of destruction means their eventual use for such purposes. We know that only the inhibitory effects of the higher centers of the brain can keep in check chaotic and destructive forces. If we do not give heed to our knowledge and create, before time runs out, a world government; if we cling to the anachronistic delusion of a defensive war or to the suicidal delusion of a preventive one—we will all slide down the well-oiled ways to Armageddon. Perhaps we can still behave like rational beings.

If mental hygiene has ever been challenged, it is challenged now.

CHAPTER XIII

New Partnerships for Psychiatry

DURING the economic depression of the thirties a certain old lady is reported to have said: "What a pity this old depression had to come just when times are so bad!" A corollary to this profound, if naïve, sentiment might be: What a pity we are in such a state of mental confusion just when the world about us seems to be tottering. Some people might prefer to state the proposition in reverse and to say that our world may be tottering because we are in a state of mental confusion.

Although psychiatrists have some notions about mental confusion, it would be vain and foolish for them to claim any special knowledge in the field of international affairs. Such knowledge as we have is fairly limited to the mental life of individuals. We know relatively little of the behavior of aggregates of people or of the laws that govern their behavior. When we deal with groups, we have a tendency to fall into the error of our own logic, logic that was once defined as "that systematic way of going wrong with confidence." We try to apply our hard-won theoretical formulations, derived retrospectively or genetically for the individual, to masses. Such applications are sometimes forced and unconvincing.

Even though in this field sociologists and cultural anthropologists move with a surer step, in method and theory they have been much influenced by the principles of dynamic psychology. In turn their discoveries are influencing psychiatry, and these disciplines are now cross-fertilizing each other. This is all to the good.

But the psychiatrist's main concern is with the individual. When confronted with such a query as: "What can modern psychiatry contribute to the United Nations?" he is, in a manner of speaking, thrown back on his haunches before he takes the jump. We are no wizards. I doubt whether we are equipped to answer all the questions that are put to us—including the sixty-four-billion-dollar one, which is: "How can the nations live together in peace and sufficiency?" Each one of us is desperately and poignantly concerned with trying to find the answer to this question.

We psychiatrists are fortunate because our private and our professional attitudes are *not* in conflict. If we were physicists, or even bacteriologists, this might not be so.

Our concern is with human beings. Even if our chief interest is in mechanisms and in discovering how the mind works, by the very methods we employ we are willy-nilly drawn into a therapeutic relationship. We are meliorists. We are always trying to make things better. We are among the legitimate heirs of Hippocrates. The fact that we are concerned with alleviating the lot of suffering man need not blunt our scientific acumen. On the contrary, it has always been a prick and a spur to our ingenuity and to our zeal for understanding.

If we ourselves are in a reasonable state of mental health, we cannot approach a sick and distraught human being with the same detachment and objectivity that a mathematician brings to his theorem or a physicist to his experiment. Since we are thus partially identified with the object of our study, we will necessarily have a bias about it. There will be a slant, a drift, a set, to our thinking. And our thinking will be influenced by the cultural environment in which we grew up and had our education. We shall not be able to approach our material without certain standards and values. The criteria for mental health we adopt, our yardsticks and our norms, are radically limited by our social history. We do not grow up in a social vacuum, and consequently we can never emancipate ourselves from our own culture. What we observe in psychiatry, as in astronomy, will be influenced by the position of the observer.

If I say that there is an American psychiatry, you will not, I hope, think me a chauvinist. Perhaps I should say, rather, a democratic one—a psychiatry that has been influenced, colored, and nourished in the democratic tradition—root and branch. And you will agree that this idea is no absurdity, as is the idea of a Nazi physics or a Nazi astronomy. It is no accident that beginning with William James and Morton Prince the concept of dynamics should have taken so firm a hold in this country and that, in spite of Freud's great prejudice against us, we overcame our prejudice against him. His focus was on the individual and on freeing him from his neurotic fetters.

If that is revolutionary, it is a revolution begun with the Magna Carta. Respect for the individual, responsibility for our acts, tolerance of others—these are the moral implications to be drawn from this dangerous doctrine—and hope and the possibility of change, and pioneering of the spirit, and conflict and dissidence, even within the individual himself. This is what we are and what our nation is. No wonder that dynamic psychiatry has flourished here in spite of parochial obscurantists who have always been the enemy of freedom and of light. And no wonder that the totalitarians have had to banish it. To them it is a dangerous doctrine because to them the individual is at once the tool and the enemy of the state.

A few years ago when the Brooklyn Dodgers sent a Negro up to bat, there was a threatened rebellion by the opposing team. The President of the National League then issued the following statement:

If you do this you will be suspended from the League. You will find that the friends you think you have in the press box will not support you, that you will be outcasts. I do not care if half the league strikes. Those who do it will encounter quick retribution. All will be suspended and I don't care if it wrecks the National League for five years. This is the United States of America and one citizen has as much right to play as another.

Compare this with the following statement written in Berlin at 4:00 P.M. on April 29, 1945, and signed by Hitler: "Above all else, uphold the racial laws in all their severity, and mercilessly resist the universal poisoner of all nations, international Jewry."

As citizens and as psychiatrists, we applaud the first statement as we condemn the second. The first means health and life for persecuted as well as for persecutor. The second means death for both. This is no theory. History has proved it so.

We come by our truths in two ways, by revelation and by experience, but even truth by revelation must stand the pragmatic test. When our hypotheses are proved wrong and are supplanted by better ones, we scrap them. This is the method of science. It is also the method of life. It holds for the principles of dynamic psychology as it holds for the principles of democratic government. In neither the one nor the other do we insist on all sharing our truths. In so far as they work for us and work well, we hope that they will be shared. But we have no legitimate objection to others proclaiming different truths—even opposing ones—so long as they do not interfere with ours. We will defend our truths against all comers until they can convince us that we are mistaken. No longer can we indulge in the luxury of complete scientific detachment. The brave new psychiatrist must roll up his sleeves.

One hundred and fifty psychiatrists recently signed a statement reaffirming the basic rights and dignity of man contained in the *Report of President Truman's Committee on Civil Rights.* The statement asserted that the protection of civil rights is vital to the mental health of our citizens; and it stressed the fact that experiences which result in frustration, insecurity, fear, and hate undermine the mental health of individuals and create unhealthy relations between persons and groups of persons.

The right to the safety and security of the person, the right to citizenship and its privileges, the right to freedom of conscience and expression, the right to equality of opportunity—these basic rights as defined in the report of the committee were proclaimed to be essential to mental health.

It is a fine thing for psychiatrists to take such a stand. But let us not be too satisfied with it. When I talk of rolling up our sleeves, I mean that, in spite of our busy lives, we should sit on school boards, take part in town councils, and bring our influence to bear on medical education and public education and industry. We must use our growing authority not only in local but in national politics. We may even be able to storm the fastness of the State Department: to sit in on deliberations such as the one on racial tensions recently held by U.N.E.S.C.O. or to act as trouble shooters at U.N. If we had some expert knowledge in human relations, we could be used to iron out misunderstandings between delegates when these are of a personal nature and are not dictated from home offices. Perhaps diplomats could get some training in psychiatry or psychiatrists some experience in diplomacy. Nothing would be lost by such an experiment, and much might be gained.

Since we psychiatrists are dedicated to the good of the individual and recognize that health is better than illness, it is easy for us to take the next step and the next and the next—easier for us than it is for scientists whose work is abstracted from notions of social good. We know that a healthy community is made up of healthy individuals, a healthy nation of healthy communities, and a healthy world of healthy nations. This is as true of mental health as of physical. Mental illness, too, spreads by a kind of contagion. It is passed on from man to man and from place to place, from generation to generation—not necessarily in the germ plasm, but in attitudes, in identifications, and in early conditioned responses.

We have every reason, therefore, to encourage and to support the world organization as an agency of the United Nations and to require that it concern itself with problems of mental health as well as physical. Although the basic sentiment of world fellowship is essential to peace, unless it is expressed in laws and in a system of government it will fail us. Here in the field of health is the natural beginning. Because here we can all agree. And we can agree with Edmund Burke when he said:

> Society is indeed a contract. . . . But the state ought not be considered as nothing better than a partnership agreement . . . to be taken up for a little temporary interest, and to be dissolved by the fancy of the parties. . . . It is a partnership in all science; a partnership in all art; a partnership in every virtue, and in all perfection. And as the ends of such a partnership cannot be obtained by many generations, it becomes a partnership not only between those who are living, but between those who are living, those who are dead, and those who are to be born.

This magnificent statement made some two hundred years ago must now be extended to include the society of nations. To the health of this partnership the modern psychiatrist will dedicate himself.

CHAPTER XIV

The Last Best Hope of Earth

MEN and women of knowledge and good will are gathered together here from many parts of the world to face their common problems, to share their thoughts, and, perhaps, also to give voice to their hopes and aspirations. We must keep the fact in mind that there can be no mental health, no world citizenship, no good group relations, so long as the nations are faced with the brutal futility of war as a method of settling their differences. The prevention of war should be our first and our chief concern. It has been said that the best way to forestall an evil is to strive for the good which is its opposite.

A citizen, as I understand it, is a person who owes allegiance to a government and is entitled to its protection. He has a responsibility as well, to develop new forms of government better suited to his needs. There is at present no world government to which we feel we owe allegiance and which can give us protection. The nations are rent by hatred, suspicion, and the constant threat of violence. Far from being citizens of a united world, we are still denizens of a divided one. And yet, there is a growing awareness among thinking men and women that, if we are to survive, we must so develop our existing outworn and inadequate nationalist states that they can become part of a transcendent organization. This is to many a remote and quixotic dream. Actually, it is the only reality. Anything else is an anachronistic nightmare, because, in the modern world, competitive sovereign states can no longer guarantee to protect the life and property of their citizens or indeed to protect them from total extermination. Almost everyone knows this in his heart, feels it, and fears it. There is a heightened awareness among us of the world's difficulties. This puts a great burden upon us and cuts off the retreat into complacency. We are forced to seek help from each other. We feel like helpless orphans bereft of protective care. There is no asylum for us just now. Can we mature sufficiently to care for ourselves? Not until we can learn also to be concerned with others, whatever the inconveniences or sacrifices we are called upon to endure.

Through man's fabulous ingenuity we are already living physically in one world. The barriers that once divided us have melted away. The seven seas do not divide us, nor do the hills of Rome, nor the wall of China, nor the Maginot Line. But as we have grown near to each other physically, we seem to be growing farther apart spiritually because our very nearness has increased the potential threat of our greed and our aggression. These have become more conscious and more menacing. They have kept us from seeing our common interests and have overemphasized our differences.

Though we are united in space, we are still epochs apart in time. Civilization has not progressed uniformly all over the world. There are parts of the earth where primitive men are held together in tribal and parochial groups bound by the narrow ties of kinship and locality. They are alien to us; just as our modern organized industrial society is alien to them. If they are laggards in the march of progress, perhaps we seem to them to have sold our birthright for a mess of gadgets. There are other peoples whose political philosophies and religious practices, whose goals and ideals, are so at variance with our own that to think that we live in the same world with them seems an unjustified extravagance. There are still others who, though dwelling in ancient and mature civilizations, almost defy a mutual understanding. Indeed, we say of all such people that they are still worlds apart from us.

What is this thing called "the world"? It is not the terrestrial globe of geography. It is no less than mankind, the inhabitants of this earth, men and women and children bound together in smaller and larger units by common origin or by tradition or habit or sometimes in pursuit of similar goals. They talk hundreds of different languages, and they worship almost as many gods. When we speak of world citizenship, do we mean that these millions are to be organized into a whole, with a governing body and courts of justice, that the citizens of this unified world will some day enjoy protection and be guarded against exploitation? Even if this is only a remote dream, its existence is what gives us heart. Though not many of us will see that bright day, the pursuit of this dream must be our daily aim.

If we are ever to unite the multifarious peoples of our planet, we can do so only in the light of their existing natures, not by wishing that they were a heavenly host of angels. They are neither angels nor devils. They are human beings with human needs, appetites, aspirations, and fears. Two properties, among many others, are common to all of them and are worth emphasizing: the tendency to gather into groups and the urge to survive. These are, of course, interrelated. The species could obviously not survive unless individuals gathered into groups. (Reduced to simple terms, this means that, with few exceptions, men and women want to continue to live on this earth, even in squalor and misery; and, with few exceptions, they will guard the lives of their offspring even at the cost of their own.)

When his survival is threatened, man quickly marshals

his defenses. Fear takes possession of him. His aggression is mobilized and his inventive genius is put to the service of protecting himself and destroying his enemy. He does not stop to think that by his maneuvers he may also be undoing himself, that in the rivalry for possession, power, and prestige the race is not always to the swift, and that the fruits of victory may turn to the ashes of despair.

According to Toynbee, nineteen of twenty civilizations have gone to their death through war or internal conflicts or some combination of the two. If we cannot learn to prevent war, then not only is civilization fated to annihilation but the human species as well. "But we are not doomed," says Toynbee, "to make history repeat itself; it is open to us, through our own efforts, to give history, in our case, some new and unprecedented turn. As human beings, we are endowed with this freedom of choice, and we cannot shuffle off our responsibility upon the shoulders of God or nature. We must shoulder it ourselves. It is up to us."

These are great words. They contain the challenge to which we must respond. What new and unprecedented turn can we give to history to insure the survival and the betterment of our civilization? I do not believe that prophecies of doom will stay our hands from self-destruction, nor will the knowledge and experience of the unspeakable horrors of modern war. It has often been said that, when warfare became sufficiently terrible and devastating, men would desist from it. Thus far this has not been so. The idea is to my mind a false reading of the motives that impel men to destroy rather than to create and, above all, to destroy what they have created.

Creation and destruction come from the same raw stuff. They are both the expression of life-force, the *élan vital* of Bergson. Whether this will assert itself in building up or in tearing down, in drawing people together in mutual confidence or in driving them apart in suspicion, fear, and hatred, is a matter for our greatest concern.

I do not believe that the good is only a "reaction formation" against the bad, that man's creative impulses are simply ways of dealing with and taming his destructive ones, that love is only an outward negation of hate. It may be true that they are made of the same raw material and stem from common drives, but that is far from saying that one is simply a negative of the other or a defense against it. A cathedral is not the same as the mass of rubble into which it may have disintegrated. Indeed, I am willing to go further than this and to assert that the constructive and cohesive forces, both in the individual and in society, will spontaneously find their way if certain limiting and constricting ones are removed, more especially fear and anxiety.

But if man has the possibility of a good life, even the will for it, why does he so frequently choose the opposite—death and destruction? It is not enough to say that he is a predatory and warlike animal or to be content with the assumption that war is the logical outcome and expression of mass aggression. Indeed, I think there is good reason to question such an assumption. Modern war could as well be blamed on the inertia of men, on their dull-witted imagination, on lack of ingenuity, resourcefulness, and planning, on belief in magic and in their own invulnerability, on miscalculation, on fear of attack—sometimes unwarranted—and, above all, on the timorous, ignorant suggestibility of masses of people.

One thing is clear, and that is that war on the grand scale cannot easily be attributed to a single cause. In this it resembles those psychosomatic illnesses that come as a culmination of a long chain of interrelated circumstances, the final breakdown of an unstable balance of forces. No matter how much one may hate the capitalist system and inveigh against it, to lay the cause of war at its door is a shortsighted oversimplification. There are economic causes, of course, and racial ones and religious ones and combinations of all of these. There are, also, ancient traditional hatreds and suspicions, outraged feelings and hurt pride. All may contribute to the final catastrophe.

It is unlikely that any simple statement can explain this enormously complicated phenomenon. That there are subjective factors at work is clear enough. These deserve our attention, partly because we have some expert knowledge in this province. Professor Theodore Abel, the American sociologist born in Poland, makes a good point when he urges the giving-up of the vain search for the causes of war and the turning instead to "a study of the *pattern* according to which a war situation develops." In this pattern the "element of decision" is an essential part. There is little evidence for the prevailing view that war begins in a kind of spiral movement of public opinion that gets out of control and ends in a stampede. This is a secondary, rather than a primary, process. But there is much evidence for believing that individuals or groups, holding some special political or economic power, lay the plans for war well in advance of the event. The group in power, when threatened, often faces the alternative of resigning or resorting to violence. The decision to engage in hostilities is based upon a careful weighing of chances; among them must be reckoned not only relative military strengths and what is now called "industrial potential" but—and this is very important from our point of view—the ability to stir up community and national sentiment.

From the examination of documents it appears that the decision to make war is reached, in most instances, from one to five years before the actual outbreak of hostilities. As examples, Abel cites the European coalition against revolutionary France, which began in 1792 but was planned at least fifteen months before; the outbreak of war between Austria and Serbia in 1914, for which the ultimatum was decided upon as early as March, 1909; and, again, Mussolini's ill-fated Ethiopian campaign, for which the date line was set a good two years before the invasion.

If this historical analysis is sound, as I strongly suspect it is, then what can we as medical and social scientists contribute to the prevention of war? This should be the real, the chief concern of our gathering. Why should we waste our time discussing world citizenship and good group relations if we cannot contribute to the solution of this problem? If we cannot do this, we might as well go home to enjoy a short reprieve and cultivate our gardens; for there will be no world for us to be citizens in, and the groups with whose good relations we are here concerned will turn into miserable, frightened, orphaned starvelings.

It seems to me unlikely that we can reach a solution to the greatest of all human problems by moral exhortation, although it is true that if all men were good the problem would not exist. We cannot conquer the great pestilences of man by shaking an admonishing finger at him and saying it is dirty and wrong to have typhus fever or bubonic plague or smallpox or malaria or yellow fever. The control of these plagues has been won by understanding their means of transmission, even before we knew the etiological agent that caused them. Just so we will not prevent war by telling men that it is foolish and nasty to fight, that they should be as brothers and love one another. For thousands of years they have been told that, and yet successive generations have fought wars, each more ferocious and more destructive than the preceding one.

We need to know more about the means of transmission of war fever, how the infection spreads, and why it is no longer a localized endemic but so quickly reaches pandemic or global proportions. We need to know how to isolate the source of infection, i.e., how to check the activities of ruthless power groups, and then to confront them with such a coalition of forces that their calculations for success will be overwhelmingly negated.

This implies a great extension and development of those democratic processes that are the only safeguards yet devised against tyrannical usurpation of power. We cannot foist those processes on countries where they are unwelcome or will not take root. We must respect other cultures and permit them to experiment. But the democracies can strive to perfect their experiment. If they do not, they will soon soften and degenerate and themselves be taken over by power groups. If they do, then they can show the world by their freedom from persecution and intolerance, by equality of opportunity and fair play, and by a high standard of living, that they have achieved a form of government in which men can live together in relative harmony. Such men will be less quickly stampeded into war. They will guard their hard-won rights, and they will combine with others to thwart an aggressor's chances of success or, if need be, to crush him.

War fever must also be controlled if we are to prevent war. The stampeding process is not, in my opinion, primarily the result of mass aggression but rather is precipitated by fear and anxiety, fear of actual invasion and destruction of homes and loved ones or anxiety induced in the masses by the group whose power is in jeopardy. Unless their homeland is endangered, most men have to be cajoled, shamed, or coerced into going to war. As they have, in the main, given up robbery and murder in their private lives, so too they do not easily lend themselves to organized killing without a good deal of provocation or preparation.

Indeed, the form and character of modern warfare does little to satisfy our aggressive impulses. For every bayonet thrust delivered there are thousands of hours spent in factories and in mines, at drafting boards and with precision instruments, in laboratories and in exhausting debate, discussion, and conferences, not to mention hours of waiting endlessly in queues and shivering miserably in foxholes. Even in the front line of attack the men who fight best are not those who hate the enmey with unbridled ferocity but those who trust and admire their commanding officers and love their messmates.

What war gives us, if not an outlet for our aggression, is a wonderful feeling of being united in a great cause. It renews our loyalty and our patriotism, and to many it holds out the illusory hope of relief from humdrum routine and domestic responsibility.

These are some of the moral equivalents that we must study to provide. In his last public utterance William James said: "The war against war is going to be no holiday excursion"; and yet I venture to say that not one simple man or woman in the world wants war, that what they want is, in Mr. Churchill's words, "a fair chance to make a home, to reap the fruits of their toil, to cherish their wives, to bring up their children in a decent manner and to dwell in peace and safety, without fear of bullying or monstrous burdens and exploitations. That is their heart's desire."

But there is no good in this world that can be gained without sacrifice. If now the nations are called upon to renounce some of their sovereignty and to unite in a world organization that works not only against war but for peace and sufficiency and health, how little of a loss is there in such sacrifice? Unless this organization is granted authority and power over and above that of its separate constituents, we shall, as Abraham Lincoln said, "meanly lose the last best hope of earth."

But we can still nobly save it. We medical and social scientists, who specialize in the study of man and his relations, must marshal all our knowledge and our best intelligence to grapple with the problem of how to prevent war, how to wall off the source of infection emanating from power groups, how to interfere at every possible point with its spread, how to build men and women who can resist these infections.

In six short days we cannot fulfil so stern an ambition, but we can make a start here and now. If the prevention of war is our steadfast goal, then we shall have a better chance of reaching an agreement on the many subjects that will come before us for study and discussion. But the world cannot be saved by scientific conferences. If it is given to us to find the right answers to some of these problems, then we must use our psychological insights to persuade statesmen and politicians to give us a hearing and to act on our findings. They would not think of trying to wage wars without the help of scientists—physical, medical, and even, now, social and psychological—but they manage to start wars which these same scientists might enable them to prevent. We must give up being isolated esoterics. We must speak a language that others can understand. If we do, they will hear us. We must join them in all humility and dedicate ourselves to the needs of mankind, with respect and reverence for the rights of other men and women, for today only a citizen of the world can be a true scientist.

Bibliography and Notes

THE author wishes to acknowledge his indebtedness to all those whose works he has consulted and to the authors and publishers who have granted him permission for the use of quotations. Their names are accompanied by an asterisk. Marginal numbers refer to page and line, respectively, of the text. Where no numbers are given, the article or book cited has a general bearing on the contents of the chapter. These were chosen not as the only authoritative sources but because the author found them useful or entertaining or sometimes even both.

CHAPTER I

THE DOCTOR'S DILEMMA

(William Root Lecture delivered before the Alpha Omega Alpha Medical Honor Society at the Medical School of the University of Rochester, March 15, 1946.)

PAGE 1, LINE 1: SHAW, GEORGE BERNARD. The doctor's dilemma. London: Constable.

PAGE 1, LINE 19: *Ibid.*, p. 12.

PAGE 1, LINE 21: *Ibid.*, p. 13.

PAGE 1, LINE 25: *Ibid.*, p. 25.

PAGE 1, LINE 25: *Ibid.*, p. 25.

PAGE 5, LINE 12: PEABODY, FRANCIS W. The care of the patient, p. 48. Cambridge: Harvard University Press, 1927.

PAGE 5, LINE 25: GOETHE, JOHANN WOLFGANG VON. Goethe and Faust: An interpretation by F. Melian Stawell and G. Lowes Dickinson. London: G. Bell & Sons, 1928.

"Man cannot learn to know a thing unless he loves it, and the deeper and fuller the knowledge is to be, the stronger, the more intense and the more living must be the love, I will even say the passion. Dislike and hatred fetter the observer: even if he has insight, they limit him to the surface. But let sympathy and love be married to insight and then the world and mankind will lie open before him: he may enter on the path which will lead him to the highest heights of all. Love is no king, it is more: it does not govern men, it makes them grow" (p. 62).

PAGE 5, LINE 27: HIPPOCRATES. Precepts. In SINGER, CHARLES J. Greek biology and Greek medicine. Oxford: Clarendon Press, 1922.

PAGE 7, LINE 4: HARTMANN, FRANZ. Paracelsus, p. 210. 4th ed. New York: Macoy & Masonic Supply Co., 1923.

PAGE 11, LINE 33: DUNBAR, FLANDERS. Psychosomatic diagnosis, chap. iv. New York: Hoeber, 1945.

PAGE 16, LINE 15: COHN, ALFRED E. Changes in public attitudes toward medicine: Historical aspects, Bull. Hist. Med., 11:12, 1942.

CHAPTER II

PSYCHOSOMATIC MEDICINE

PAGE 17, LINE 4: MARAT, JEAN PAUL. Philosophical essay on man: Being an attempt to investigate the principles and laws of the reciprocal influence of the soul on the body: A history. London: Ridley, 1773.

PAGE 17, LINE 9: ZILBOORG, GREGORY. Psychosomatic medicine: A historical perspective, Psychosom. Med., 6:3–6, 1944.

PAGE 17, LINE 15: OBERNDORF, C. P. The psychiatric novels of Oliver Wendell Holmes. New York: Columbia University Press, 1943.

PAGE 17, LINE 18: EDES, ROBERT T. New England invalid, p. 57. Boston: David Clapp & Son, 1895.

PAGE 17, LINE 24: PUTNAM, JAMES JACKSON. Not the disease only, but also the man. The Shattuck Lecture; delivered at the annual meeting of the Massachusetts Medical Society, June 13, 1899. (Medical communications; also Collected papers of James J. Putnam, 1:1–33.)

PAGE 17: COBB, STANLEY. Psychosomatic medicine, Harvard M. Alumni Bull., 20:50, 1946.

PAGE 18, LINE 3: DRAPER, GEORGE. Disease, A psysomatic reaction, J.A.M.A., 90:1281, 1928.

PAGE 22, LINE 8: CANNON, WALTER B. Bodily changes in pain, hunger, fear and rage. 2d ed. London: Allen & Unwin.

——. The wisdom of the body. London: Kegan Paul.

PAGE 24, LINE 18: ALEXANDER, FRANZ. The influence of psychologic factors upon gastrointestinal disturbances: A symposium, Psychoanalyt. Quart., 3:501, 1934.

PAGE 24, LINE 26: WOLFF, HAROLD G., and WOLF, STEWART. Studies on a subject with a large gastric fistula: Changes in the function of the stomach in association with varying emotional states, Tr. A. Am. Physicians, 57:115, 1942.

PAGE 24: WOLF, STEWART, and WOLFF, H. G. Human gastric

function: An experimental study of a man and his stomach. New York: Oxford University Press, 1943.

PAGE 25: BINGER, CARL. The doctor's job, chap. ix. London: Allen & Unwin, 1947.

PAGE 26, LINE 6: DUNBAR, FLANDERS. Psychosomatic diagnosis, chap. iv. New York: Hoeber, 1945.

CHAPTER III

THE MIND AND THE HEART

The author wishes to thank Dr. Robert O. DuBois and Dr. Mack Lipkin for their helpful comments on the first part of this chapter.

PAGE 28, LINE 11: WOLF, G. A., JR., and WOLFF, H. G. Studies on the nature of certain symptoms associated with cardiovascular disorders, Psychosom. Med., 8:293, 1946.

PAGE 41, LINE 12: LEVINE, M. An orientation chart in the teaching of psychosomatic medicine, Psychosom. Med., 10:111, 1948.

PAGE 42, LINE 18: BOAS, E. P. Personal communication.

PAGE 43, LINE 14: WOLFF, H. G. Protective reaction patterns and disease, Ann. Int. Med., 27:944, 1947.

PAGE 43, LINE 21: MITTELMANN, B., and WOLFF, H. G. Affective states and skin temperature: Experimental studies of subjects with "cold hands" and Raynaud's syndrome, Psychosom. Med., 1:271, 1939.

PAGE 43, LINE 24: SMITH, H. W. Physiology of the renal circulation, Harvey Lect., 35:166, 1939–40.

PAGE 43, LINE 27: WOLF, S.; PFEIFFER, J. B.; RIPLEY, H. S.; WOLFF, H. G.; and WINTER, O. S. Hypertension as a reaction pattern to stress: Summary of experimental data on variations in blood pressure and renal blood flow, Ann. Int. Med., 29:1056, 1948.

PAGE 44, LINE 10: BINGER, C. A. L.; ACKERMAN, N. W.; COHN, A. E.; SCHROEDER, H. A.; and STEELE, J. M. Personality in arterial hypertension, Psychosom. Med., Monographs. New York, 1945.

PAGE 44, LINE 12: LOFTUS, T. A.; GOLD, H.; and DIETHELM, O. Cardiac changes in the presence of intense emotion, Am. J. Psychiat., 101:697, 1945.

PAGE 44, LINE 14: GOLD, H.; KWIT, N. T.; and MODELL, W. The effect of extracardiac pain on the heart, A. Research Nerv. & Ment. Dis., Proc., 23:345, 1943.

PAGE 44, LINE 26: WORTIS, S. B. Personal communication.

CHAPTER IV

Psychotherapy in Arterial Hypertension

Page 46, Line 11: Goldblatt, H. Studies on experimental hypertension; production of the malignant phase of hypertension, J. Exper. Med., 67:809, 1938.

Page 46, Line 26: Page, I. H., and Corcoran, A. C. Arterial hypertension: Its diagnosis and treatment, p. 16. Chicago: Year Book Publishers, 1945.

Page 47, Line 20: Alexander, F. Psychoanalytic study of a case of essential hypertension, Psychosom. Med., 1:139, 1939; and Emotional factors in essential hypertension, ibid., p. 173.

Page 47, Line 21: Menninger, K. A. Emotional factors in hypertension, Bull. New York Acad. Med., 14:198, 1938.

Page 47, Line 21: Moschowitz, E. Hypertension: Its significance, relation to arteriosclerosis and nephritis and etiology, Am. J.M. Sc., 158:668, 1919.

Page 47, Line 21: Rennie, T. A. C. The role of personality in certain hypertensive states, New England J. Med., 221:448, 1939.

Page 47, Line 21: Saul, L. J. Hostility in cases of essential hypertension, Psychosom. Med., 1:153, 1939.

Page 47, Line 21: Weiss, E. Psychosomatic aspects of hypertension, J.A.M.A., 120:1081, 1942.

Page 47, Line 22: Binger, C. A. L.; Ackerman, N. W.; Cohn, A. E.; Schroeder, H. A.; and Steele, J. M. Personality in arterial hypertension, Psychosom. Med., Monographs. New York, 1945.

Page 51, Line 7: Weiss, E. Personal communication.

Page 51, Line 34: Hill, L. B. Psychoanalytic observation on essentional hypertension, Psychoanalyt. Rev., 22:60, 1935.

CHAPTER V

Learning from a Medical History

Page 58, Line 9: Wolff, Harold G. Protective reaction patterns and disease, Ann. Int. Med., 27:944, 1947.

Page 58, Line 17: Shakespeare, William. Hamlet, Act II, scene 1.

Page 62, Line 7: Deutsch, Felix. Associative anamneses, Psychoanalyt. Quart., 8:354, 1939.

CHAPTER VI

The Concerns of Psychiatry

Page 66, Line 8: Grinker, Roy R., and Spiegel, John P. War neuroses in North Africa: The Tunisian campaign; January–May 1943, p. 17. New York: Josiah Macy, Jr., Foundation, 1943.

——. Men under stress. Philadelphia: Blakiston, 1945.

Menninger, William C. Psychiatry in a troubled world. New York: Macmillan, 1948.

Menninger, William C., and Leaf, Munro. You and psychiatry. New York: Scribner, 1948.

Rennie, Thomas A. C., and Woodward, Luther E. Mental health in modern society. New York: Commonwealth Fund, 1948.

CHAPTER VII

Anxiety

Page 78, Line 5: Darwin, Charles. The expression of the emotions in man and animals, pp. 237–40. New York: Appleton, 1899.

Page 78, Line 25: Cannon, Walter B. Bodily changes in pain, hunger, fear and rage: An account of recent researches into the function of emotional excitement. London: Appleton, 1922.

Page 80, Line 4: *Sitwell, Sir Osbert. Autobiography.

Page 83, Line 13: Shakespeare, William. Hamlet, Act II, scene 2.

Page 83, Line 26: Freud, Sigmund. The problem of anxiety, p. 99. New York: Norton, 1936.

Page 84, Line 9: Freud, Anna, and Burlingham, Dorothy T. Young Children in War Time. London: Allen & Unwin, 1942.

Page 84, Line 9: ———. Infants without families. London: Allen & Unwin, 1944.

Page 87, Line 32: "Normopath": This term was invented by my friend, Professor Victor von Weizäcker of Heidelberg.

CHAPTER VIII

Psychoanalysis

Page 89, Line 17: Freud, S. The basic writings of Sigmund Freud, p. 934. New York: Random House, 1938.

Page 90, Line 5: Goldsmith, Margaret. Franz Anton Mesmer: A history of Mesmerism. New York: Doubleday, Doran, 1934.

PAGE 90, LINE 22: Ibid., pp. 154–55.
PAGE 90, LINE 34: FREUD, op. cit., p. 934.
PAGE 91, LINE 14: Ibid., p. 943.
PAGE 92, LINE 29: HENDRICK, IVES. Facts and theories of psychoanalysis, p. 4. New York: Knopf, 1944.
PAGE 93, LINE 34: FREUD, SIGMUND. Collected papers, 2:316. London: Hogarth Press, 1924.
PAGE 96, LINE 16: HENDRICK, op. cit., p. 47.
PAGE 97, LINE 22: RADO, SANDOR. The relationship of patient to therapist, Am. J. Orthopsychiat., 12:541, 1942.
PAGE 97, LINE 33: HENDRICK, op. cit., p. 208.
PAGE 98, LINE 10: Ibid.
PAGE 102, LINE 25: KUBIE, LAWRENCE S. Practical aspects of psychoanalysis, p. 206. New York: Norton, 1936.
PAGE 102, LINE 35: HENDRICK, op. cit., pp. 238–48.
PAGE 104, LINE 4: Ibid., pp. 256–57.
PAGE 104, LINE 9: FREUD, S. The basic writings of Sigmund Freud, op. cit., p. 965.
PAGE 104, LINE 12: Ibid., p. 939.

ALEXANDER, F. The medical value of psychoanalysis. Rev. ed. New York: Norton, 1936.
———. The indications for psychoanalytic therapy, Bull. New York Acad. Med., 20:320, 1944.
BINGER, CARL. The doctor's job, pp. 55–73 London: Allen & Unwin, 1947.
DEUTSCH, H. Psychoanalysis of the neuroses. Translated by W. D. ROBSON-SCOTT. London: Hogarth Press, 1932.
FREUD, SIGMUND. The psychopathology of everyday life. Translated by A. A. BRILL. London: T. Fisher Unwin, 1914.
———. Introductory lectures on psycho-analysis. Translated by JOAN RIVIÈRE. London: George Allen & Unwin, 1929.
———. New introductory lectures on psycho-analysis. Translated by W. J. H. SPROTT. New York: Norton, 1933.
OBENDORF, C. P. Consideration of results with psychoanalytic therapy, Am. J. Psychiat., 99:374, 1942.
SAUL, L. J. Physiological effects of emotional tension, personality and the behavior disorders, 1:269. Edited by J. McV. HUNT. New York: Ronald Press, 1944.

CHAPTER IX

WHAT IS MENTAL HEALTH?

PAGE 118: BINGER, CARL. The doctor's job, p. 59. London: Allen & Unwin, 1947.
PAGE 118, LINE 34: JONES, ERNEST. The concept of a normal mind, Internat. J. Psycho-Analysis, 23:7, 1942.

PAGE 119, LINE 12: BRIDGES, ROBERT. Testament of beauty. London: Oxford University Press, 1929.

PAGE 120, LINE 29: BERNARD, CLAUDE. Leçons sur les phénomènes de la vie communs aux animaux et aux vègétaux, 1:50. Paris: Baillière, 1878.

PAGE 120, LINE 33: CANNON, WALTER B. The wisdom of the body. London: Kegan Paul.

CHAPTER X

ON CHOOSING A MATE

PAGE 130, LINE 4: Successful marriage, chap. ii, The wise choice of mate by ERNEST W. BURGESS,* pp. 17–31. Edited by MORRIS FISHBEIN and ERNEST W. BURGESS. Garden City: Doubleday, Doran, 1947.

PAGE 134: SAUL, LEON J. Emotional maturity. Philadelphia: Lippincott, 1947.

CHAPTER XI

WHY THE PROFESSOR FELL OUT OF BED

(First published in abridged version in Harper's Magazine for October, 1947.)

PAGE 139: KUBIE, LAWRENCE S. Elements in the medical curriculum which are essential in the training for psychotherapy, p. 46. Vide infra, Josiah Macy, Jr., Foundation, 1947.

PAGE 139, LINE 24: PORTER, W. C., and DAVIDSON, H. A. Alumni appraisal of psychiatric education, Am. J. Psychiat., 103:440, 1947.

PAGE 140, LINE 32: WHITEHORN, JOHN C. Psychiatry in medical education: The teacher–characteristics and qualifications, Am. J. Psychiat., 103:446, 1947.

PAGE 146, LINE 30: CORWIN, E. H. L. The American hospital. New York: Commonwealth Fund, 1946.

PAGE 151, LINE 6: Training in clinical psychology, transactions of the first conference, March 27–28. New York: Josiah Macy, Jr., Foundation, 1947.

PAGE 151, LINE 24: MENNINGER, KARL A. Psychiatry and psychology, Bull. Menninger Clin., 11:45, 1947.

PAGE 151, LINE 24: MENNINGER, KARL A.; RAPPAPORT, DAVID; and SCHAFER, ROY. The new role of psychological testing in psychiatry, Am. J. Psychiat., 103:473, 1947.

PAGE 156, LINE 7: SPITZ, RENÉ A. Hospitalism, an inquiry into the genesis of psychiatric conditions in early childhood, The Psychoanalytic Study of the Child, 1:53. International University Press, 1945.

CHAPTER XII

Medical Information and Misinformation

Page 160, Line 19: *Sitwell, Sir Osbert. The scarlet tree, p. 41. London: Macmillan.
Page 163, Line 31: Flesch, Rudolf. The art of plain talk, p. 6. New York: Harper,* 1946.
Page 164, Line 34: Hayakawa, S. I. Language in action, pp. 233–34. New York: Harcourt, Brace,* 1941.
Page 165, Line 31: Ibid., p. 75.
Page 166, Line 8: Chase, Stuart. The tyranny of words, p. 63. New York: Harcourt, Brace,* 1938.

CHAPTER XIII

New Partnerships for Psychiatry

Page 172, Line 2: Becker, Carl L. How new will the better world be? p. 7. New York: Knopf, 1944.
Page 175, Line 1: To secure these rights: The report of the President's Committee on Civil Rights, p. 19. Washington, D.C.: United States Government Printing Office, 1947.
Page 175, Line 11: Trevor-Roper, H. R. The last days of Hitler, Hitler's "Political Testament," pp. 179–82. London: Macmillan, 1947.
Page 177, Line 18: Burke, Edmund. Reflections on the Revolution in France. 1790.
Levy, David M. New fields of psychiatry. New York: Norton, 1947.

CHAPTER XIV

The Last Best Hope of Earth

(Abridged version of the opening address delivered at the International Congress on Mental Health held in Central Hall, London, August, 1948. Published in the American Scholar, winter number, 1948–49.)

Page 181, Line 15: Toynbee, Arnold J. Civilization on trial, p. 39. New York: Oxford University Press, 1948.
Page 183, Line 14: Abel, Theodore. The element of decision in the pattern of war. Am. Sociological Rev., 6:853, 1941.
Page 186, Line 22: James, William. The moral equivalent of war, A. Internat. Conciliation, Leaflet No. 27. 1910.
Page 186, Line 25: Churchill, Winston. Speech at Congress of Europe, The Hague. May 7, 1948. (As reported in the New York Herald Tribune, May 8, 1948.)

Index

For Product Safety Concerns and Information please contact our EU representative GPSR@taylorandfrancis.com Taylor & Francis Verlag GmbH, Kaufingerstraße 24, 80331 München, Germany